GHOSTS OF THE BELLE ÉPOQUE

GHOSTS OF THE BELLE ÉPOQUE

A History of the Grand Hôtel et des Palmes, Palermo

by
Andrew Edwards &
Suzanne Edwards

TAURIS PARKE
Bloomsbury Publishing Plc
50 Bedford Square, London, WC1B 3DP, UK

BLOOMSBURY, TAURIS PARKE and the TAURIS PARKE logo are trademarks of
Bloomsbury Publishing Plc

First published in Great Britain in 2020

A catalogue record for this book is available from the British Library

ISBN: HB: 978-1-838-60388-5; eBook: 978-1-838-60389-2

2 4 6 8 10 9 7 5 3 1

Typeset in Perpetua by Deanta Global Publishing Services, Chennai, India
Printed and bound in Great Britain by CPI Group (UK) Ltd. Croydon, CR0 4YY

To find out more about our authors and books visit www.bloomsbury.com
and sign up for our newsletters

CONTENTS

LIST OF ILLUSTRATIONS

To our dear families

———————

'Homeward Bound'

I have been to every tavern
Running up and running down,
And of every surly waiter
Made inquiries in the town.

Lo, I see her in yon window!
And she beckons all is well!
Could I guess that you had chosen,
Lady, such a grand hotel?

Heinrich Heine

PALAZZO INGHAM

The sensuous warmth of a June evening in Palermo was exacerbated by an intense heat radiating from flaming torches that lined the Marina, past the Porta Felice to La Cala. Nobles with wealth enjoyed the night air from the ostentation of their carriages; a nod or a wave to those that mattered was sufficient to ensure their presence had been acknowledged. As the crowds filtered through the imposing stone gate named after Donna Felice Orsini, a former Viceroy's wife, groups of people congregated, exchanging gossip and opinions. These flambeaux in the summer of 1808 were a rare sight for young Benjamin Ingham from Yorkshire.

Flames from the torches illuminated the face of sixteen-year-old Estina Fagan, the Anglo-Italian daughter of Robert Fagan, portrait painter, archaeologist and, later, British Consul-General of Sicily. Benjamin from Ossett was captivated. The twenty-four-year-old Ingham cultivated the image of a dandy, styling his hair in the fashionable 'first consulate' manner which required a feathered fringe to fall loosely over his eyebrows and lengthy sideburns to brush his cheeks. His urbane appearance however hid a flinty, matter-of-fact character; Ingham was no poet but a hard-headed businessman. His efforts to court the beautiful Estina included excursions with the Fagan family to the orange and lemon groves of Bagheria and Monreale but would go no further due to her family's desire for a wealthier match. They had already chosen William Baker, whose grandfather was Governor of the Hudson's Bay Company and director of the East India Company, the heir to a kind of wealth that young Benjamin could only dream of attaining.

Despite the fact that he came from a prosperous Yorkshire family, by 1806 — two years prior to his first glimpse of Estina Fagan — Ingham had lost virtually everything, both in love and business. As well as working as a representative for the family business, he had been carrying on his own trading ventures, but owing to the vagaries of Georgian sea travel had seen his investment sink to the bottom of the ocean when the ship carrying precious cargo was caught in a storm. His romantic life followed suit when his fiancée Anne Brook broke off their engagement, perhaps not wanting to marry a luckless merchant. The city of Leeds and his family home in Ossett, a market town near Wakefield, no longer held the promise and fascination of former years. When the opportunity arose to travel to Sicily with the intention of selling cloth on behalf of the family business, he did not hesitate.

Ingham's arrival coincided with feverish British activity on the island in a bid to keep the Mediterranean open for naval operations during the Napoleonic Wars. By 1806, British troops had landed, a move welcomed by many of the local aristocrats and by the royal family, who had fled to Palermo from Naples after Napoleon deposed King Ferdinand (styled both Ferdinand III of Sicily and Ferdinand IV of Naples) and installed his own brother as king. These were tumultuous times but, for the quick-witted entrepreneur, there were many opportunities. English trader John Woodhouse had become a fortified wine baron after establishing a winery in Marsala on Sicily's west coast. Admiral Nelson's favourite sherry was off-limits due to the Napoleonic blockade and Woodhouse's Marsala ably filled the gap. It was not long before Benjamin Ingham visited Marsala and saw the huge potential that the product held for future business.

In 1812 Ingham set up his own winery, known locally as a *baglio*, in direct competition with John Woodhouse, after sending his brother Joshua on a clandestine fact-finding mission to Spain to copy the best techniques used by the sherry houses. Ingham had no desire however to live in provincial Marsala and he decided that the only place for a man of his would-be stature was Palermo. John Woodhouse, on the other hand, portrayed himself as a man of strict morality, despite rumours of repressed homosexuality; he saw the Marina with its *flambeaux*, fêtes and festivities as the height of depravity, especially when the torches

were extinguished after midnight creating, as contemporary travel
writer Patrick Brydone noted, an ambience 'better to favour pleasure
and intrigue'.

The most titillating affair of all was the relationship between Admiral
Lord Nelson and Emma Hamilton, the wife of Ambassador William
Hamilton. Emma was a noted beauty who had achieved a certain *succès de
scandale*. Pryse Lockhart Gordon, an author and former acquaintance of
Lord Byron, arrived in Palermo when the famous couple were resident.
After docking he went immediately from the harbour to be presented
to Nelson and to William Hamilton; however, he was somewhat keener
to meet the Admiral's mistress, as his account indicates:

> Our introduction to the fascinating Emma Lady Hamilton was an
> affair of more ceremony, and got up with considerable stage effect.
> When we had sat a few minutes, and had given all our details of
> Naples, which we thought were received with great *sang-froid*, the
> Cavaliere retired, but shortly returned, entering by a *porte battante*,
> and on his arm or rather his shoulder was leaning the interesting
> Melpomene, her raven tresses floating round her expansive form
> and full bosom.

Gordon took apartments in the Palazzo Patrollo, off the Marina, and
was delighted with the 'extended terrace forty feet wide and sixty in
length, looking full on the bay'. His *Personal Memoirs* return again to
Lady Hamilton during one particularly eventful ambassadorial dinner.
A Turk who had fought at the Battle of the Nile, a famous victory
of Nelson's, claimed in a drunken slur that he had despatched many
Frenchmen with the sword he was currently wearing to the dinner, and
duly produced the blood-encrusted weapon. Emma Hamilton took the
sword from his hand, kissed it, and passed it to Nelson. Gordon was
shocked by such a brazen act, as was the Consul-General's wife who
fainted at the scene.

British writers of the time were both fascinated and shocked by Sicilian
attitudes to sex and marriage. The Hamilton *ménage-à-trois* would have
provided little novelty to an aristocracy used to such arrangements. The
Reverend Brian Hill in his 1791 book, *Observations and Remarks*, gives us

this somewhat pious opinion on the state of Sicilian marital relations: 'The crime of adultery is so common that no Dame of rank is thought the worse for being guilty of it.'

Benjamin Ingham's love-life, although not worthy of Gordon's pen, was also far from straightforward. As his business interests flourished and Estina became a distant memory, he integrated further with the island's high society. By 1819 he had formed a relationship with Alessandra Spadafora, the Duchess of Santa Rosalia (1778–1851), who became his mistress. Alessandra already had four sons from her marriage to the Duke Pietro Ascenso, who was to die at sea in a battle against the Turks in 1821. From the chronology, we can see that an affair had already begun before the unfortunate Duke's death. Only one of the Duchess' children was in a stable financial position, having married an heiress. The others were spendthrifts, who would come to rely on the largesse of Ingham. He was not noted for suffering fools gladly, but was surprisingly indulgent with Alessandra's sons; such generosity did not extend to his own nephews employed in the business.

Alessandra, in the way of many Sicilian aristocrats, had a string of titles to her name. In addition to being a duchess, she was Princess of both Venetico and Maletto, Marchesa of San Martino and Roccella, and also the Baroness of Mazara. A photographic portrait exists of an aged Alessandra wearing a voluminous black dress and a very dour expression. Raleigh Trevelyan, the author of *Princes under the Volcano*, an invaluable resource for anyone interested in the history of the Ingham-Whitakers in Sicily, says that Ingham's wider family considered the Duchess 'a tartar' whose formidable temper was equal to that of her lover. She was always trying to manoeuvre her sons into a favourable position that would see them inherit some of Ingham's wealth. Naturally, Benjamin's blood relations looked upon such machinations less than sympathetically.

The first of Ingham's nephews to arrive in Sicily was William Whitaker (1796–1818), ostensibly summoned to work in the family firm as Ingham had initially, although it was clear his uncle was grooming him to take on responsibilities in his expanding business empire. William was pitched into the rocky economic territory of post-Napoleonic War Sicily. In the recession of 1816, Ingham was trying to juggle more than just the various facets of wine production; he had been dealing in olive oil and sumac, and had also diversified into the more traditional Yorkshire rag trade and bill broking. He would go on to pull many other operations into his all-encompassing vortex, including sulphur and shipping. William would have found Ingham at his home in Via Bara, neighbouring the Lampedusa family who would spawn Giuseppe Tomasi di Lampedusa, the author of *The Leopard*, a novel that captures the twilight of Sicilian aristocracy during the Garibaldi invasion.

The house in Via Bara All'Olivella, to give the street its full name, was both a home and a headquarters — a complete contrast from the as-yet-to-be-constructed pleasure palace of the Palazzo Ingham which would become the 'Grand Hôtel et des Palmes (The Palms)'. Modern-day Via Bara is a relatively constricted thoroughfare bisecting the main avenue of Via Roma. Rather than being tarmacked, it is diagonally paved with substantial stones worn smooth with the passing of much traffic, both pedestrian and vehicular. In places, the street narrows to such an extreme that two cars travelling in opposite directions would be likely to clip wing mirrors or meet in a stand-off. The several storeyed, once grandiose, buildings face each other, balcony to balcony, their paint peeling and plaster flaking.

Lampedusa remembered Via Bara as a squalid and poor area but, as Raleigh Trevelyan points out, it must have been a rich and mercantile address in the days of Benjamin Ingham. A sense of the Ingham era can be felt where the street intersects with Via di Lampedusa. The Palazzo Branciforte has been renovated to become an exhibition centre, and its elegant white façade with ochre trim and imposing entrance archway, complete with mock portcullis, speaks of the power once wielded by the Branciforte family. Opposite is the less imposing, but equally smart, Palazzo Lampedusa. Little remains of the interior captured so beautifully by Lampedusa in his memoir, *Places of my Infancy*. During our initial visits in the first decade of the twenty-first century, the palazzo was in a very sorry state. An American bomb during World War II had reduced it to ruin with little hope of revival. It took savvy property developers to resuscitate the exterior, the price being its conversion into apartments. A quick search on the internet will show that these are currently for sale, at doubtless exorbitant prices.

Benjamin Ingham sent William Whitaker forth from Via Bara to negotiate on behalf of the firm. One of his first assignments was to investigate two firms in Naples with which Ingham was doing business, and which were in financial difficulty. Much to the irascible Ingham's ire, William disappeared for longer than was expected. His eventual apology and explanation revolved around a complicated power of attorney and a desire not to worry his uncle. The truth of the matter, however, had more to do with the attractions of a raven-haired Neapolitan beauty called Clotilde. Sadly, just as the young man was settling in to his Italian routine and adjusting to life with his uncle, he was struck with a fever and died in November 1818.

Ingham is famously quoted as having written to his sister saying that 'Your son is dead. Send me another.' This apocryphal request seems incredibly harsh, even for the blunt Yorkshireman; the actual letters concerning his nephew's death show a far more tender appreciation of a life so prematurely cut short. The replacement was William's brother Joseph Whitaker (1802–84), a man perfectly suited to the job of administrative functionary for a demanding boss. He had a scrupulous hold on the purse strings, both for the firm and his own household. Sophia, his wife, is said to have remarked, rather wistfully, after Joseph had died, that she would have loved to have owned a brooch. The delights and fripperies of Palermo society held no attraction for Joseph, who would beaver away at the office, putting in all the hours required. When he returned home for dinner, he demanded complete silence whilst eating his food, so an acquiescent Sophia would sit demurely to one side as the *paterfamilias* digested his meal. There must have been some highlights in the marriage, however, as they had twelve children in regular succession.

As we know, even the taciturn Ingham allowed himself the best that Palermo had to offer. He became fluent in Sicilian, not just the standard Italian used for business across the peninsula, and through the good auspices of his Duchess he was able to participate fully in the island's aristocratic life. He made the sound decision early on to trust the locals in business, an attitude conspicuous by its absence in the majority of expatriate merchant circles. Consequently, he was accepted as an equal by even the haughtiest of Sicily's nobility.

Despite such assimilation, one area in which he refused to compromise was religion. Surrounded by Catholics, he remained a staunch Protestant. The Ingham family had a proud ancestry in matters spiritual. His namesake Benjamin Ingham, born in 1712, was a preacher attracted to the Moravian Methodist philosophy who wrote *A Discourse on the Faith and Hope of the Gospel*. His followers were known as Inghamites and they set up chapels in his name — some still exist today. Although our Benjamin did not go to these extremes, he was always happy to meet and greet Protestant clergy.

The theologian, poet and Anglican priest John Henry Newman (1801–90) who would, ironically, go on to convert to Catholicism, gives us an insight into Ingham's kindly attitude and lifestyle at the time. Cardinal Newman, as he would become, had made the mistake of travelling alone through Sicily's interior. He was struck down with illness near to the central city of Enna and recuperated at one of the town's inns. Before these trials and tribulations, he had made his way to Palermo where he was invited to dine with Ingham. Newman did not record his opinion of Alessandra Spadafora, but was much taken with the 'splendid' food, in addition to indulging his priestly palate with 'two or three glasses of wine'.

Newman returned to Palermo after his enforced sojourn in Enna, only to find that he could not return home to England because there was no vessel available. Raleigh Trevelyan is sure that the intervention of Ingham provided a passage on a French ship going to Marseille. Even then, the vessel was becalmed for a week between Sardinia and Corsica, providing the cleric ample time to write his famous hymn, *Lead Kindly Light*.

Sicily did not feature heavily on the Grand Tour itinerary, unlike its sister in the Bourbon monarchy, Naples. However, a few intrepid and less holy Grand Tourists made the trip, especially after the Scotsman Patrick Brydone had published his successful journal, *A Tour through Sicily and Malta*, in 1773. Part of the attraction was the road less travelled and an escape from gawking fellow countrymen who were wickedly satirised by the Irishman Thomas Moore in his 1819 poem, 'Rhymes on the Road': 'And is there then no earthly place, / Where we can rest, in dream Elysian, / Without some cursed round English face, / Popping up near, to break the vision!'

That being said, the few aristocrats who crossed the Tyrrhenian Sea were relieved to find hospitality offered by Ingham and his fellow merchants, even if their hosts were touched by the indignity of having to work for a living. The advantage of a meal with Ingham was the *entrée* he could provide into Sicilian society. Such connections were deemed important, as well-to-do Sicilians had become somewhat wary of travelling nobles, precisely because Brydone, a travelling companion to the idle rich, had revealed too many of their secrets in print. Most of those from the higher echelons of British society who bothered with the island left little in the way of written impression; one notable exception was John Butler, titled Lord Ossory and later the Second Marquess of Ormonde. Ingham was rather scathing of the young buck's tendency to overindulge in late-night carriage rides up and down the Marina, forgetting his own early fascination with the spectacle.

Ormonde's 1850 Sicilian memoir, *An Autumn in Sicily*, published years after his travels, paints a vivid picture of early nineteenth-century Palermo and gives an insight into his own stereotypical bias. He stayed in the Hotel Marletta on Via Toledo, which is now Via Vittorio Emanuele; it was a comfortable residence but did not reach the heights of The Palms during the Belle Époque:

> The Toledo attracts attention from the number of very long latticed balconies on each side, belonging principally to religious establishments, who add to their means by letting them to spectators of the great religious processions which annually take place. The royal palace stands at the inland end of the street Il Cassaro, a name derived from the Arabic *al kasr* (the palace). The thoroughfares are full of mendicants, whose appeals for charity are vociferous and unceasing; and the bustle in them caused by the antagonism of real business and determined laziness and lounging, though amusing at first, becomes wearisome when curiosity is once satisfied. Along the sea runs a very fine promenade, La Marina, whence there is a fine view of the bay, and which forms the favourite resort of all the rank and fashion of the town.
>
> Signor Marletta's hotel, where we found a very good accommodation, is situated at one end of the Toledo. Adjoining it is

a large prison, which is somewhat of a drawback to its comfort, as, independently of the disagreeable importunity for charity of those confined in it, to which the inmates of the hotel are subject every time they appear in the street, the nightly hailing of the sentinels to each other every half-hour is tiresome in the extreme, and renders it desirable to secure a bed-room as far removed as possible from their neighbourhood.

Unfortunately, Ormonde never tells us if he secured a residence which he would have considered more befitting his station, but he does elaborate on the entertainments he enjoyed with the city's *beau monde*. Although he thought the opera to be inferior to that of Naples, he was more than happy to attend regularly, specifically visiting the box held by the Principessa Partana whom he considered to be at the centre of Palermo's social whirl. According to the Marquess, the society 'was agreeable and easy'.

He also met Baron Pisani, a fascinating character, who typified the fact that some Palermitani used their position in society for more than mere fripperies. Pisani had created la Real Casa dei Matti, a home for those suffering with mental health problems that was a world away from the grim asylums of the day. This is Ormonde's description of a meal taken at the institute: 'We saw them all at dinner, which consisted of soup, meat, bread, grapes, and a small allowance of wine, served in a most comfortable way. All possible liberty is allowed to them, and the old-fashioned methods of restraint are nearly unknown.'

Pisani's method was so innovative that esteemed publications in North America were commenting on his vision and practice. The Boston Medical and Surgical Journal of 1835 had this to say:

This plan of treatment, so efficacious and humane, for the cure of insanity, is a proof of the superior mind of him, under whose directions it has been carried into effect; and although it would be very difficult to find such an estimable person to superintend similar establishments, the plan here described will be found more and more advantageous and satisfactory, as it is judiciously employed. The labors [sic] and ingenuity of the worthy Baron may thus, in some measure, be imitated; but who, we may ask, will imitate the indefatigable constancy with which he has pursued his painful and arduous undertaking?

The Baron even encouraged the therapeutic use of music and theatre, in addition to the advantages of gardening, as Ormonde noted. The patients tended the plants which included some rare species such as the papyrus reed, more commonly associated with Syracuse in the south-east of the island. It is perhaps no coincidence that it was the Boston medical press who came to hear of Pisani's revolutionary approach to mental health. There were strong connections in the business world between Palermo and Boston, many of which were fostered by Benjamin Ingham himself.

In 1823 Benjamin had called yet another nephew, Joseph Ingham (1803–33), to Palermo. His namesake, Joseph Whitaker, was productively ensconced in the office at Via Bara and his uncle needed someone to look after his interests in Marsala. However, the sombre Joseph Ingham was not suited to the atmosphere he found in the town and soon found himself severely criticised by his sharp-tongued uncle. Joseph was summarily packed off to Boston to look after the company's North American interests, which included the transportation from Sicily of sumac, pumice, cloth and, of course, wine. In return, his nephew was to arrange for the export of American wood to be made into wine casks. Sadly, only a few years later Joseph Ingham's American odyssey came to an end when he shot himself in a New York hotel. He was said to have been suffering from depression, or melancholia, as it was termed in the nineteenth century.

During Joseph's Boston years, his two younger brothers had also decided to make long-term futures in Palermo. Benjamin Ingham Jr., fortunately known as Ben, and Joshua Ingham saw the family firm as gainful employment. Although an adopted Palermitan at heart, Ben would be the one chosen to ping-pong between America and Sicily, after he was sent to Boston initially to sort out the complications that had arisen over Joseph's will. Raleigh Trevelyan reports that Ben stayed for many months to further the business and was so successful that he became an itinerant frontman for the company.

The arrival of two more nephews and the strength of the North American arm were both factors in the consolidation of the business during the 1830s. Benjamin Ingham Senior's thoughts now turned to his relationship with the Duchess of Santa Rosalia. Some mystery surrounds the legalisation of his liaison with Alessandra. Did he actually marry her? It was known in the family that Uncle Benjamin had intentions of formalising his partnership, much to their dismay. Nothing is known of the ceremony and, given she was Catholic and he was Protestant, it was likely to have been a civil arrangement. The non-existence of any record means that the legality of the marriage has been called into question. Historians have made the point that he did not take any of her titles, which would have been useful assets on an island so heavily populated with abundant *principi* and *baroni*, although he did become the Baron of Manchi e Scala, an estate he owned in central Sicily.

Further intrigue revolves around a comment made many decades later by Tina Whitaker, the wife of Joseph Whitaker Jr., who was the son of Benjamin's nephew, Joseph. Tina had a side-line in writing and penned a pamphlet on Ingham's life entitled *Benjamin Ingham of Palermo*. Rather casually, she made the claim that Benjamin had ensured that Alessandra sign away any claim on his fortune before their marriage took place. If this is to be believed, such a document would be a very early example of a 'pre-nup'. Once again, no record exists and the family were still clearly worried about their chances of inheritance after Alessandra supposedly became Mrs Ingham.

Whether or not Alessandra achieved official status, she seems to have participated more fully in the required social aspects of Ingham's business affairs after their formalised relationship. She was, however, anything but punctilious and was, in that respect, a polar opposite of the regimented Ingham, who liked deadlines to be met and meetings to take place at their allotted time. Alessandra had the *laissez-faire* attitude of an aristocrat used to taking life at her own pace, and on one specific occasion, being dilatory actually worked in her favour.

In 1840, to appease Alessandra, who hated visiting Marsala, Ingham had bought a country estate nearby, called Racalia. The surrounding countryside, during periods of scarcity, was infested with bandits. One of Sicily's wealthiest men travelling with his noble wife would have been fair game and a prize beyond belief. The robbers had heard whispers in Marsala that the party would be making the short journey to Racalia and, therefore, had decided to lay in wait. Alessandra was running so late that she delayed their departure for days. Baking under the sun in the flatlands behind the port with eyes constantly focussed on the track, the mind-numbing tedium and frayed nerves finally got the better of the would-be highwaymen and they decided that even the Englishman's riches were not worth the wait.

Racalia was not the only property that Ingham would reside in after the pseudo-marriage. The couple finally moved from Via Bara, leaving it to Joseph and Sophia Whitaker, and settled in Piano di Sant'Oliva to the north-west of their old residence. The new Villa Ingham was elegantly balanced and designed to match its Palermitan neighbours. The area stretches from Piazza Castelnuovo by way of Piazza Sant'Oliva, along Via Carini to Via Porta Carini. The house on Castelnuovo no longer exists and has been replaced with a glass-fronted commercial block which looks towards the bandstand built by Joseph Whitaker's son. The nearby triangular Piazza Sant'Oliva is more verdant, softened with a neat hedge-lined park planted with oleander. The paths of this small public garden lead to the bust of Giuseppe Pitrè, the Palermitan professor and folklorist who was born in 1841, just as the Inghams were finding their feet in a new district. Pitrè would go on to write *Sicilian Fairy Tales, Stories, and Folktales* and even set up a department for folklore at the University of Palermo.

The professor, in his capacity as a collector of the island's fables, would have been aware of the many stories attributed to the hardship of the sulphur industry. The workers, known as *zolfatari*, suffered dreadfully with lacerations on their sallow skin and deteriorating eyesight, all the more heartbreaking when we learn that some were mere children. In our literary guide to Sicily, we discussed the written representations of such mining, foremost of which was Nobel Laureate Luigi Pirandello's 'Ciaula scopre la luna' ('Ciaula discovers the moon'). In this short story Ciaula, a young miner's helper, develops a fear of natural darkness above ground, being more used to the enveloping gloom of the mineshaft.

Another representation of mining which helps us to appreciate the sheer desperation of such an occupation comes from the pen of Giovanni

Verga, the renowned Catanese realist who was born a year before Pitrè. In his short story 'Rosso Malpelo' ('Nasty Redhead'), taken from *Novelle siciliane (Sicilian Stories)*, the eponymous protagonist with the flaming hair is institutionalised in the mine, along with the poor animals who accompany him:

> ... he seemed perfectly adapted to that line of work, even in the color [sic] of his hair and those mean cat's eyes which blinked if they saw sunlight. It's the same with the donkeys that work in the pits for years and years without ever coming out again; they're lowered by ropes into those passages where the entrance shaft is vertical, and they remain there as long as they live.

Ingham must have been aware of the appalling conditions endured by the miners, but it seems not to have affected his decision to invest in sulphur. In the first half of the nineteenth century, Sicily had a virtual monopoly on the world's supply of the mineral. This 1840 text, *Review of the Neapolitan Sulphur Question*, rather suspiciously anonymised with the authorship attributed to 'A British Merchant', details the extent to which the British had begun to monopolise the sulphur trade, owing to a boost in demand from northern industry:

> In 1825, the import duty on sulphur, in Britain, was reduced from £15, per ton, to 10s. per ton... These circumstances gave at once an immense impetus to the demand for sulphur, in branches of manufacture in which it had not previously been employed; chiefly, however, in the production of alkalies [sic] for the use of the soap and glass makers. Thus, in the case of soda, by the addition of sulphuric acid to common salt, a crystallizable [sic] sulphate of soda is produced ...

The 'Concern', as the Ingham-Whitakers called their company, was riding this wave of expansion until the King of the Two Sicilies, Ferdinand II, gave in to French pressure and in 1838 granted an exclusive licence to the French firm of Taix, Aycard from Marseille. This marked an end to the favourable terms experienced by merchants from Britain and had an immediate and detrimental effect on trade. The following year, Westminster sent the Secretary of the Board of Trade to the Neapolitan court to 'catechise and coerce' the King. His argument stated that Ferdinand had broken the Treaty of Commerce signed in 1816. Sicilian sulphur was making big news in the House of Lords as can be seen from this speech by Lord Lyndhurst, reported in the *Review of the Neapolitan Sulphur Question*:

> The terms of the contract with Taix & Co. he contended, was in direct violation of the treaty of 1816, as it compelled the British merchants settled in Sicily either to sell the produce of their mines to Taix & Co. or in the event of their choosing to export it on their own account, they had to pay a duty to the Neapolitan Government.

The Foreign Secretary, Lord Palmerston, now exchanged furious notes with Ferdinand, and the British fleet was sent to blockade Naples in an attempt to stop any sulphur passing through the port. The British navy used the rather sneaky technique of flying the colours of a third nation, only to reveal the Royal Navy ensign when they boarded the Neapolitan vessels to check for the mineral. By way of response, the King sent 12,000 troops to Sicily. The so-called 'Sulphur War' was beginning to escalate to such a degree that there was a danger of conflict. Our anonymous merchant shows the disdain felt by the English in Palermo for Ferdinand and his advisors:

> The argument of such persons, as maintained, in reply to all this vituperation, that the King of Naples had, as an independent Sovereign, the unquestionable right to devise and promulgate whatever fiscal regulations he thought advisable with respect to his own dominions, continued to be treated with the utmost scorn and contempt.

Ingham was one of the 'settled merchants' referred to by Lord Lyndhurst, and he must have been extremely relieved when the French government intervened to try and broker a solution. The Taix contract was cancelled and the monopoly rescinded. However, the British Consul-General, in late 1841, was still noting considerable discontent amongst mine owners and merchants due to the fact that the punishing duty had been left in place. A petition was sent to Naples, although as the Consul-General notes, the only British name amongst the irate Sicilians was none other than Benjamin Ingham.

Ingham distracted himself from the sulphur crisis by dabbling in pepper importation. It was in his ship *Elisa* that the first cargo of pepper ever to be transported directly from the East Indies to the Kingdom of the Two Sicilies arrived in Palermo. Prior to the success of this venture, all trade in the spice had involved third parties and other countries. Ingham was fêted by Palermitan society, and the King temporarily put aside his ill-concealed dislike for the British and invested Benjamin with the Order of Saint Ferdinand.

Pepper was much more common than it had been in the Middle Ages, yet it was still a luxury item around which there was much mystique. Aside from its obvious use as a flavouring and a condiment, it was thought to have healing properties. Black pepper was put to use in treating everything from constipation and insomnia to abscesses and toothache. One of its more unusual medicinal applications was in the calming of sunburnt skin, something the northern aristocracy who had started to visit Palermo would no doubt have appreciated if caught unawares by the strength of the sun. Contrary to the badge of honour the modern holidaymaker gives to a bronzed body, a pale complexion was favoured by anyone who considered manual labour under the sun as beneath them.

Although not attracted by the summer's excessive rays, the nobility were starting to see the winter's relative heat as a tonic. The local circles in which Ingham moved were set alight by the arrival of the Tsarina Alexandra in 1845, after her physician had recommended warmer climes. By this stage in her life, the already-frail Tsarina was suffering from a nervous twitch which developed into convulsions of the head. Although Tsar Nicholas I was reluctant to have his wife spend so many months in Sicily, he conceded, on the premise that he would pay a brief visit. It is endearing to think that his reluctance was due to the romantic notion of a husband missing his wife, but less so when we learn that he could not bear to leave for Sicily without taking his mistress along for the journey.

Alexandra stayed in the Villa Butera in Bagheria, now a twenty-minute car ride from Palermo. In the nineteenth century Bagheria was the key destination for the *villeggiatura* — the annual escape from the city favoured by the nobles and their families. Many built splendid villas amongst the orange and lemon groves. A large percentage of these aristocratic holiday homes have survived but are now hidden by the chaotic urban sprawl of concrete, traffic and decaying industry. The most renowned of all Bagheria's villas is the one that once belonged to the Prince of Palagonia, whose sister was the first wife of the Duke of Santa Rosalia, the former husband of Benjamin Ingham's Alessandra.

Palagonia surrounded his villa with a high wall that he decorated with hundreds of chimerical statues which gave rise to its local nickname, the Villa of the Monsters. Hunchbacked gnomes follow human-headed horses ridden by cherubs and the twisted body of an effete musician looks towards a writhing, contorted gargoyle. Surely these must have been born from a very disturbed mind, although the Comte de Borch in his *Lettres sur la Sicile et sur l'île de Malthe* (*Letters on Sicily and Malta*) found the Prince 'just and correct in his reasoning about everything'. Not so the two Hamburg psychiatrists Helen Fisher and Wilhelm Weygandt, who, according to Giovanni Macchia in his book, *Il principe di Palagonia,* posited the theory that he built the monstrous statues in a bid to exorcise his own ugliness.

Interestingly, the author Rosanna Balistreri has seen method in the madness. Her 2008 book *Alchimia e archittetura* (*Alchemy and architecture*) suggests that the Villa Palagonia subscribes to an alchemical pattern. She has noticed the proliferation of musicians on one side of the central building and chimerical statues on the other. Looking over this progression is the god Mercury, who represents the transmutation of matter, the heart of alchemy. Balisteri's theory concludes that this is a search for harmony, starting from the ethereal nature of music and finishing with a tangible subject.

Such a unique and fascinating building has not failed to draw the attention of writers and poets, and both Patrick Brydone and Wolfgang Goethe brought the Villa Palagonia into the consciousness of northern Europe. The architecture promotes passionate responses whether negative or positive. Goethe, steeped in the classicism of Greece and

Rome, was affronted by the monstrous abandon; however there is an unsubstantiated rumour that Salvador Dalí, the Spanish surrealist, had once declared a desire to buy the villa for vacations in Sicily. It certainly would have suited his theatricality. Fortunately, the villa remains partly inhabited by locals and is open to visitors. Ingham and his nephews would have visited the gardens and house on numerous occasions; sadly, they have left no record of their impressions amongst the plentiful letters housed in the family archives.

By 1851 Benjamin Ingham was beginning to reduce his personal involvement in the Concern. He nominally retired, although in practice he was never able to completely relinquish the reins. He had more time for leisure, but the fripperies of Bagheria were never enough to tempt him to build in the environs. Ingham and the Concern had survived through turbulent times including a cholera outbreak, the sulphur debacle, brigandage and even the 1848 uprising against the Bourbon monarchy, the precursor to events in 1860 that would change Italy forever. It was time for Benjamin to enjoy his wealth a little. Villa Ingham in the Piano di Sant'Oliva was now witness to some incredibly lavish parties attended by the upper echelons — everyone from the powerful General Filangieri to the Valguarnera, Lampedusa, Butera and Niscemi families, many of whom, in the way of close-knit aristocracies, were related.

Filangieri was the officer who had led Ferdinand II's troops into Palermo to finally quell the 1848 uprising. The Ingham-Whitakers had feared greatly that he would employ the slash-and-burn tactics he had used in villages on the outskirts of the city. However, he was more prudent in the capital and directed his attention towards those intent on wanton destruction. In the years to come, he would also prove to be one of the few Neapolitan administrators liked by the Sicilians. The reason behind Filangieri's invitation to the Duchess of Santa Rosalia's social functions was, as indicated by Raleigh Trevelyan, her desire to achieve a pardon for her son. Carmelo Ascenso, now the Marquess of Roccella, had swapped sides during the revolution and become a colonel of the Sicilian forces, defending the castle of Taormina.

Post-conflict parties were grandiose affairs, often requiring the men to be decked out in full regimental regalia and the women to elegantly style themselves in the voluminous skirts of silk ballgowns. A glimpse of the setting for such occasions can be captured by turning to Lord Byron's former publisher, John Murray, who had been producing a series of travel handbooks. Little remains in print of these extravagant balls, but the villa is mentioned in *A Handbook for Travellers in Sicily*, written by George Dennis (1814–98) and published by the aforementioned Murray. The guide briefly describes the art hanging on Ingham's wall:

> The Palazzo Ingham, on the Monte di Santa Rosalia, contains a very fine picture by Pietro Novelli, one of the latest from his hand, and formerly in the possession of the Prince of Maletto. It represents the Trinity commanding the archangel Gabriel to announce the mystery of the Incarnation to the Virgin.

Maletto was Alessandra's brother and she had inherited all his furnishings. It is not clear whether Dennis had mistakenly upgraded Villa Ingham to a palazzo – itself a question of semantics – or if he was referring to the palazzo that Ingham commissioned in 1856.

Deciding that Sant'Oliva was now too small, Ingham bought a parcel of land from the Prince of Radali who, like him, was a foreigner acclimatised to the island. Radali was Ernst Wilding, the Earl of Königsbrück, who hailed from a branch of the Hanoverian Wilding family that had previously married into the Sicilian Buteras. Money for the land exchanged hands in England and Ingham set about building his new home, the future Palms Hotel. There is no historical record to confirm whether the site already contained a building, but we do know that Ingham's palazzo had two storeys with seven balconied windows – fewer floors and windows than the current configuration. It also boasted the famous glasshouse that would be removed when the architect Ernesto Basile was asked to renovate the building in the early twentieth century.

The edifice fronts Via Roma and is sandwiched between Via Mariano Stabile and Via Principe di Granatelli. The area outside the entrance used to be known as Piazza Ingham or even, in the mouths of rough-and-ready Palermitani, English Square. Abutting the structure was Via Ingham, a nomenclature that has long since disappeared.

However, a wider search of the map reveals that Benjamin Ingham is still commemorated with a street name in the Roccella district of Palermo. It is a far cry from the salubrious surrounding of The Palms, being a long strip of road bordered by rather tedious commercial and industrial outlets; although perhaps this is fitting for such a business-minded individual.

Stepping from the hotel today, the visitor is presented with a view that is a world apart from its original outlook. The square once had a plethora of tropical trees and plants, including the ubiquitous, eponymous palm and the more exotic monkey puzzle. Ingham had moved a short geographical distance from the Marina of his twenties where he had gazed in fascination on the lamp-lit amorous assignations of local nobles, but had made a huge leap in his personal and professional status. When people spoke of banking and business in Sicily, they spoke of Benjamin Ingham. As late as 1957, Ingham was still being touted as a man of consequence in Harvard's *Business History Review*, where Irene D. Neu wrote about his life in the article, 'An English Businessman in Sicily'.

Throughout the 1850s revolutionary ideas continued to circulate, as did the dreaded cholera, killing approximately 24,000 people in Palermo in 1854. Eventually, the epidemic subsided but notions of liberation from the Bourbon yoke did not. In the last year of the decade, Ferdinand II died and was succeeded by Francis II whom Tina Whitaker, in her book *Sicily and England*, calls 'vacillating, weak and priest-ridden'. The high-society gatherings were increasingly a cover for meetings of a different kind where plots were hatched and war materiel hoarded. The time had come for Giuseppe Garibaldi (1807–82) and his 'spedizione dei Mille' (Expedition of the Thousand). Maybe Ingham thought that this uprising would be one more failed attempt at upsetting the status quo, as Neu describes: '... old Benjamin Ingham, in Palermo, unaware that he was seeing the end of an era, closed the shutters of his house, prepared to wait out what he was sure would be just another unsuccessful revolution.'

Garibaldi landed with his thousand rebels, the so-called 'Redshirts', in Marsala in May 1860. Guiseppe Cesare Abba, one of the General's contingent, wrote his account of the military manoeuvres in *The Diary of*

One of Garibaldi's Thousand. His description of the troop disembarkation and exchange of fire is very evocative:

> All of a sudden, there was a cannon shot. What's that? 'Only a salute,' said Colonel Carini, smiling. He was dressed in a red tunic with a great broad-brimmed hat on his head, with a feather stuck in it. A second explosion and, with a roar, a large cannon ball came bouncing between us and the seventh company, throwing up the sand as it went. The street-urchins throw themselves to the ground, the friars bolt — as well as they can with their gross bodies, waddling along in the ditches. A third ball crumples up the roof of the near-by guard-house. A shell falls into the middle of our company and lies smoking ready to explode. Beffagna, the Paduan, rushes to it and draws the fuse. Bravo! But he neither hears nor cares.

Abba noticed that some of the *bagli* and villas of Marsala were flying foreign flags, mostly English, in an attempt to inform both sides of their presence, thus avoiding destruction from the shelling. Ingham's warehousing and properties escaped serious damage, as did his interests in Palermo, although it was a close-run thing, as this report from British officer Lieutenant Wilmot demonstrates. Wilmot had been sent to the Palazzo Ingham by Admiral Rodney Mundy, whose ship *Hannibal* had entered Palermo harbour on a mission to assess the situation and to protect British interests:

> With much difficulty I found my way to Mr Ingham's house, which is situated on the western outskirts of the town, near the English gardens. The damage done throughout this district is very great, especially in the neighbourhood of Garibaldi's headquarters ... The shells were still falling, and several times I had to shelter myself in a doorway till they exploded. It was also very unpleasant crossing the Toledo and streets facing the Palace and Mint, as the troops were constantly firing down them with musketry and field-pieces. Close to Mr Ingham's house there had evidently been a severe struggle. I saw several Royal artillerymen and horses dead, and still remaining where they had fallen.

As Garibaldi had moved from Marsala to Palermo, he had picked up bands of local supporters on the way. Momentum was shifting in favour of the Redshirt rebels. As Algernon Sidney Bicknell relates in his contemporary account *In the Track of the Garibaldians Through Italy and Sicily*, the time was over-ripe for a lasting revolution: 'That which enfeebled the Bourbon government so much as to cause it ultimately to collapse before a mere handful of desperate men, was the spirit of disaffection kept alive in the servants of the state by the perpetual insurrectionary outbreaks of the Sicilians.' His retelling of the events in Palermo chimes alarmingly with Wilmot's account above, as the besieged Bourbon troops sought a bitter form of refuge in certain key buildings:

> In an instant, the whole city was an enemy's camp for the garrison; no valour in the streets, even if they had displayed it, could have availed them now; some retreated to the Palace and others to the Castle. Then ensued from the guns of both these places a murderous bombardment of the defenceless town, while ships of war, anchored off the Marina, threw shells indiscriminately in every direction, crushing the houses and burying whole families in their ruins.

In advance of Garibaldi, the island had already been infiltrated by certain key supporters of the Risorgimento, amongst whom was Francesco Crispi (1818–1901), who had been exiled from Ribera, a town in the south-west of Sicily. Crispi would go on to spend much time in The Palms espousing his political philosophy to willing acolytes; however, for the time being, Garibaldi's advance meant that at last he could divest himself of the ludicrous disguises he had adopted as a covert agent. *The New York Times* reported that he had been able to obtain counterfeit passports matching his spurious identities, one of which was a Latin-American tourist complete with *bandido* beard and glasses.

Crispi was a friend of both Garibaldi and Giuseppe Mazzini, one of the key activists in Italian unification, in addition to being a shrewd political operator. When he saw that the wind was changing direction in favour of unification, he abandoned the notion of a completely independent Sicily and took up the cause of Italian nationalism. Many Sicilians saw a unified country as a means of obtaining a degree of autonomy via separation from the hated Bourbons. The poor of the countryside were more inclined to view the revolutionary fervour in terms of an opportunity to shake off the remnants of feudalism and obtain some degree of land reform. Whether any of these goals met the giddy heights of expectation is open to question. A large percentage of modern Sicilians feel they have swapped one distant master for another, thereby repeating the seemingly endless cycle of the island's history.

To avoid the conflict, Benjamin's nephew Ben Ingham and his wife slipped away to England en route to America. The Whitakers took advice from the British navy and boarded a ship anchored in Palermo harbour. The now-aged Benjamin was however less inclined to move from his residence, preferring to sit out the shelling. Bicknell tells us that the British consul had to endure nineteen hours of missiles flying over his roof; his house was directly in the line of fire between the port and the palace. An armistice was called, after which the Neapolitans officially yielded to the invading troops. Crispi cobbled together a government and Garibaldi turned his focus towards the mainland. The foreign merchants were left in limbo, reliant on the decisions of the fledgling administration.

One effect of the power vacuum was a reassessment of religion. In Naples, a certain Padre Gavazzi dressed himself in extravagant raiment and proceeded to rename churches at will to equate the new movement with the rising of Christ. He was eventually chased off by an angry mob; nevertheless, the British Bible Society saw an opportunity to evangelise and set up wooden stalls along the length of the city's Via Toledo, selling Italian translations of the Bible and giving away pamphlets full of Protestant content. They had very few takers, apart from curious and concerned priests who would occasionally pick up a leaflet in order to judge the opposition. We have found no reference to the Society performing a similar task in Palermo, although it would be easy to envisage the same evangelists attempting to roll this very large stone uphill towards Monte Pellegrino, Palermo's most imposing landmark. Bicknell was under no illusion that such interventions were futile: 'I do not know whether the Society sent the brochures as well as the books, but they were about the last things in the world calculated to do any good in a Catholic country, being vulgar in title and violent in language.'

Despite the proto-government's attempts to plan for a new future, the immediate concern was security. Previous uprisings had led to aimless disorder when troops were disbanded and the Risorgimento was no different. Palermo suffered from considerable lawlessness but the worst incident occurred in Bronte, the Duchy inherited by Nelson's family. Nelson never visited the town, being just one more absentee landlord, a situation with which the island was so familiar. Lady Bridport, the incumbent during Italian unification, had also left a bailiff in charge. The peasants saw the victory of Garibaldi as a chance to improve their lot and grab some land. During a demonstration, matters descended into chaos and lasted for days. Rioters lit fires and murderous gangs turned on property owners leaving a trail of corpses in their wake. Garibaldi, who wanted to keep the English on side, sent his fearsome right-hand man, General Nino Bixio, to put down the revolt — which he achieved through casual brutality.

History has not viewed Bixio's behaviour well and it has proved an embarrassment to Garibaldi's efforts. The town theatre and municipal archives were lost in the firestorm of retribution and the final insult was a kangaroo court with summary executions of the supposed ringleaders, the latter event earning Bixio the title 'the Butcher of Bronte'. Ingham, however, with his hard-headed business sense, was in no doubt about the efficacy of the general's approach — a method he felt should be adopted in other provinces, and said as much in a letter to the British consul John Goodwin.

Benjamin Ingham's final years were spent in an environment of violence and unrest, a backdrop common to much of his life on the island. Considering that there were several periods during which business activity was all but suspended, it is remarkable that he was able to accrue such enormous wealth. His attitude to Bixio highlights the cold tenacity required to survive and thrive in such turbulent times. The family was all too aware that Ingham's demise must be imminent, although he was showing no signs of illness, and they were jostling for position in the high-stakes game of his last will and testament. The Duchess continued to push forward her own sons, whilst Joseph Whitaker's considerable brood felt their familial bloodline should hold sway, not to mention Joseph himself, and his cousin Ben. The other nephew in the firm, Joshua Ingham, had died in 1846.

Il barone, the grand old man of Sicilian business, finally died on 4 March 1861 at the age of seventy-six, most probably of a heart attack. Raleigh Trevelyan details the machinations and peculiarities that followed his death. It seems that Ingham may have had a last-minute change of heart with regard to his will. Trevelyan tells us that he threatened to nominate as his heir a new candidate, the marvellously named Theophilus Hastings Ingham, who hailed from the religious wing of the family back in Yorkshire; however, Theophilus, inexperienced in Sicilian matters, was not to inherit. An altered will was never found and so the bulk of the inheritance went to William Ingham Whitaker, the son of Joseph. The now bald and be-wigged Duchess of Santa Rosalia was allowed to live at the firm's expense in the Sant'Oliva house and her sons had all their considerable debts repaid. Joseph Whitaker continued in his position at the head of the firm, having been left the banking enterprise and the house in Via Bara.

Joseph's son, known by all as Willie, could not take advantage of the entirety of his inheritance until he reached the age of twenty-five or until he married — craftily, he was to marry before that age. There is a mystery in the will with regard to the Palazzo Ingham because it receives no mention whatsoever. Trevelyan gives the plausible explanation that the land acquired by Benjamin was, at the time, purchased in the name of his nephew, Ben. This supposition is based on the fact that Ben and his wife, Emily, took up residence soon after the Baron's demise.

Ingham was originally buried in the Lazzaretto Acquasanta cemetery until it was closed down, after which his remains were removed to the Protestant Cimitero Acattolico ai Rotoli, otherwise known as the Vergine Maria. It can be found to the north of Arenella on the south-east coast of Sicily. His grave, under the shaded protection of a venerable tree, is topped by a monument that carries a circular urn with a central cross embellished by filigree floral relief work. This cylinder sits on a hexagonal plinth which bears the inscription: 'In memory of Benjamin Ingham Esquire, Cavaliere del Real Ordine di S. Ferdinando e del Merito, who departed this life March 4th A.D. 1861 aged 76 years'. Fittingly, the wording is both in English and Italian.

The burial ground had been a gift from Garibaldi to James Rose of the British community in recognition of his support during the uprising. Although the Protestants now had a consecrated cemetery, they were still worshipping at the British Consul-General's residence, and it took the collective decision of Ben and Joseph to change this situation. In 1871 they announced their decision to jointly fund the building of an Anglican church for residents and visitors. The site chosen was opposite the Palazzo Ingham across the piazza, now rechristened Square Emilia in honour of Ben's wife. Other Protestant residents also made financial contributions and the architect William Barber, later assisted by Joseph's son-in-law Henry Christian, was appointed to make the design.

The building, begun in 1872, took three years to complete and is characteristic of Anglican churches of the period. An enormous rose window, the key decorative feature, looks out over the arched doorway towards the square. The offset bell tower rises sharply to a point and is topped with a wrought iron cross. Italian texts on the churches of Palermo draw attention to the building's lack of adornment, and when one considers the golden interiors of La Martorana, the Palatine Chapel and the Cathedral at Monreale, La chiesa della Santa Croce (the Holy Cross church), stands out for its simplicity.

The Ingham-Whitakers were keen to reach their new place of worship without having to sully themselves by crossing the busy thoroughfare in front of the Palazzo. The solution was a secret passageway connecting the church to their residence. The corridor still exists and is hidden behind a large gold-framed mirror in The Palms' Blue Room (Sala Azzurra). Needless to say, this concealed conduit was used for more urgently clandestine purposes during World War II.

Whitaker family members were administrators for the church right up until 1962 when control was completely handed to the Diocese of Gibraltar in Europe — the Anglican Church's largest administrative area which covers not only continental Europe, but also Morocco, Turkey, parts of the Soviet Union and even Mongolia. Documents relating to the history of the building, however, are held by the Fondazione Giuseppe Whitaker, the Palermo foundation instituted in 1975 in honour of Joseph 'Pip' Whitaker, Joseph's ornithologist son.

Sadly, Ben Ingham was never able to appreciate the completed church or the finished renovations to the Palazzo which he had commissioned for his wife, Emily. Ever the itinerant businessman fashioned by his Uncle Benjamin, he was in Paris during October 1872, dining at the Hotel Meurice, when he began to choke. In a few short hours he was dead at the age of sixty-two. It would not take Emily long to re-marry, choosing to accept a proposal from Giacomo Medici, famed for his role in capturing the South Tyrol from the Austrians. At the time he was Palermo's Prefect, one who was keen to apply his militaristic bent to law and order. He was also convinced that infrastructure was the key to Sicily's development. He oversaw the laying of much rail track and it was during his rule that the Palermo to Trapani train line was opened.

The new Signor and Signora Medici chose not to live in Palazzo Ingham, making the decision to sell the property in 1874, the year after Giacomo relinquished control of the Prefecture. The buyer was Enrico Ragusa (1849–1924), son of Salvatore Ragusa, the legendary proprietor of the Hotel Trinacria. The Trinacria, still extant but no longer catering for tourists, is situated in Via Butera. Prior to The Palms, it was the city's premier hotel and the site of Garibaldi's 1862 speech declaiming 'Rome or death'. A plaque on the wall reads: '*Giuseppe Garibaldi al grido di "Roma o morte" partì per l'impresa che pur troncata ad Aspromonte ravvivava la fede affrettava gli eventi*' ('Giuseppe Garibaldi, to the cry of "Rome or death" set out on the mission which, although cut short at Aspromonte, would revitalise belief and hasten events'). It commemorates the Battle of Aspromonte that saw Garibaldi injured and stopped in his first attempt to march on and capture Rome for the newly unified Italy.

The Trinacria was also chosen by Giuseppe Tomasi di Lampedusa as the location for the death of the Prince of Salina in his book *The Leopard* (see chapter 5). Salina sits on the hotel balcony looking out to sea and breathes his last in metaphorical waves, a complete contrast to the inert Tyrrhenian Sea before him. In reality, the hotel was a favourite of British officers and those spirited enough to venture south from Naples on their own more contemporary version of the Grand Tour. Trevelyan mentions a Mr and Mrs Moens accompanying a party of voluble Americans from Marseille in 1865. They headed for the Trinacria and were relieved to find that Salvatore Ragusa was well-tuned enough to the needs of fussy

northern Europeans to turn away from his *table d'hôte* an unfortunate
Sicilian who 'expectorated incessantly'.

In more recent years, part of the former hotel was converted into
a convention centre. It was at a 1992 conference about the judicial
system that the two anti-mafia judges, Giovanni Falcone and Paolo
Borsellino, leant towards each other, smiling, in a private fraternal
moment. The affecting tableau was caught on film by the photo-
journalist Tony Gentile, and has become an iconic image in light of
their heartbreaking assassination by the mafia within a few months
(see chapter 6). A mural reproduction of this photograph now adorns
the wall of a building overlooking the Palermo yacht marina — just a
stone's throw from the Trinacria.

The Ragusa family were obviously steeped in the hospitality industry
and it is clear that Enrico wanted the chance to forge his own path in the
trade. The sale of Palazzo Ingham was the perfect opportunity to make
his own mark in the city and create an establishment with even grander
pretentions than those of his father. The reported price was 20,000 lire, a
mere drop in the ocean when we learn that Ingham's Italian estate on his
death amounted to more than £8,000,000. This is a considerable figure
in itself today, but would be eye-watering if converted to a modern-day
value. Nevertheless, it was a significant sum for Enrico, especially as
he was not content with the basic configuration and immediately spent
more money adding to the layout, a task he would repeat in 1882 with
a further expansion. The garden of the Palazzo provided the perfect
inspiration when it came to naming his new establishment. He opted
for cosmopolitan French, baptising it the 'Grand Hôtel et des Palmes', a
protracted title quickly shortened by the Palermitani to the *delle Palme*,
and known in English as 'The Palms'.

2

TRACES OF WAGNER

Cavaliere Ragusa, to give the new proprietor his somewhat dashing title, was initially a reluctant hotelier. He was just fourteen when his father, Salvatore, made the decision to send him to Berlin for the purpose of learning the family trade. He attended a school that specialised in the hotel business where he gained a more than passing acquaintance with French, English and Russian, as well as the German in which his lessons were conducted.

Back in Sicily at the tender age of twenty, Ragusa was ready to take on the running of establishments in Catania and Agrigento. The southern city of Agrigento was beginning to cash in on the fashion for touring ancient sites. Its Greek ruins, although heavily reconstructed, are among some of the most spectacular examples outside of Greece itself, so Ragusa's business was naturally called 'L'Hotel des Temples'. The establishment of The Palms, at the heart of Sicily's capital, was an obvious progression and a flamboyant sign of his success. Running such a prestigious hotel in his twenties made the entrepreneur quite a catch, and he caught the eye of Lucia Salvo Cozzo di Pietraganzili, a young Marchioness. Unfortunately, she died at the age of only twenty-seven in 1887, just ten years into their marriage, leaving him to look after their six children. Their relationship, however, opened to Ragusa the corridors of power and the salons of culture.

Both of these avenues were useful to a man who was not just obsessed with commerce. The sojourn in Berlin had also stimulated Ragusa's interest in the study of butterflies and other insects. Three years prior to establishing The Palms, he had met Baron Arthur Leopold Rottenberg, who had come to Sicily with the express aim of studying all things entomological, a meeting which prompted Ragusa to join the Società Entomologica Italiana (Italian Entomological Society). Ragusa was assiduous in collecting specimens, which he dated and geographically pinpointed for the society. It seems that the hotelier also had a keen eye for recognising specimens and describing them for the scientific community. Although he did not come from an academic background, Ragusa became friendly with those responsible for the entomological section of the zoological museum.

By 1881 Ragusa had become so well-known in the world of the study of the island's natural sciences, having also made friends and acquaintances in the fields of geology, malacology and botany, that he decided to found a monthly magazine called *Il naturalista siciliano: giornale di scienze naturali* (The Sicilian Naturalist: Journal of Natural Sciences). We can see from the introduction labelled 'To the readers' in the edition from 1 October 1881 that Ragusa and his editorial team were upbeat about scientific progress and the island in general: 'Alongside the vigorous economic development taking place in Sicily, there is a lively intellectual reawakening, and parallel to the growth in industry and commerce is an increase in the love of the arts, letters and scientific study.'

The introduction also lists the specialisms of the magazine's major contributors. The importance of Ragusa's aristocratic connections can be seen by the fact that two of the seven names listed were marquises — the Marchese Allery di Monterosato in charge of the study of shells, and the Marchese Antonio De Gregorio Brunaccini dealing with geology. Naturally, Ragusa was the entomologist. For this edition, he wrote an article entitled 'Coleotteri nuovi o poco conosciuti della Sicilia' ('The lesser-known new coleoptera of Sicily'). The piece starts with the activity he loved the most, hunting down his specimens in the field. A nod is given to his inspiration, Baron Rottenberg:

One July, years ago, whilst out hunting between Palermo and Mondello, I caught on the sand, near the sea, a beautiful variety of littoralis, having a third off-white spot on each elytra, united with a fifth which is closest to the suture of the elytra, forming the shape of a seven.

Poor Baron Rottenberg also found this variety in a single specimen, and with the seven only on the left elytra, mentioning it in his piece on the coleoptera of Sicily (Beri, Ent. Zeit. 1870) — not giving the name, but only saying that Schaum cites it. Mr René Oberthur, the fortunate purchaser of Baron Chaudoir's magnificent collection of carabidae, wrote to me having found it in said collection with the name var. lugens Dahl.

Clearly, Ragusa had stretched his self-taught passion beyond the concept of mere amateur hobbyism. He uses the term 'poor' to refer to Rottenberg because the unfortunate Baron died before he could realise his full potential as an entomologist. Not so Ragusa, who saw his magazine fire the interests of both serious amateurs and career academics. His day job as hotel proprietor was also very useful in facilitating the visits of foreign specialists, notably the renowned Austrian coleopterist Edmund Reitter and the French lepidopterists Jean-Baptiste Eugène Bellier de la Chavignerie and Pierre Millière.

The 1883 publication *Catalogo ragionato dei coleotteri di Sicilia* (The Annotated Catalogue of Sicilian Coleoptera) could be considered Ragusa's masterwork, as it echoes down the decades and continues to provide a point of reference for the modern-day entomologist. Some of his specimens of beetles and butterflies also still exist, most importantly the collection of lepidoptera sold to Lionel Walter Rothschild which is now in London. Other specimens can be found as far afield as Budapest or more locally in the Biological, Geological and Environmental Sciences department of Catania University.

When not out in the field in pursuit of rare species, normal life encroached on Ragusa with all its complications. It is fair to say that the editors of *Il naturalista siciliano* skated over some of the less palatable facts when they lauded the island's economic and cultural developments. Sicily was in a state of flux and the lobby of The Palms soon became a meeting place for those concerned with the complexities of Sicilian society. As evidenced by the various uprisings and general disorder, the Risorgimento had not created the sunlit uplands of stable Sicilian autonomy so desired by the majority of the rich and poor alike. Those at the forefront of Garibaldi's movement were now faced with some significant dilemmas: how to provide stability and the opportunities promised whilst placating the opposing factions. Francesco Crispi believed himself to be up to the challenge.

The hotel provided the perfect backdrop for Crispi's sense of theatricality which, as we know, had once manifested itself in the ridiculous guises he had adopted as a covert agent prior to the arrival of the Redshirts. He was a Sicilian of complex origin, descending from Albanians who had fled the Adriatic coast during the aftermath of Scanderbeg's defeat by the Ottomans in 1468. The exiled Albanians, known as the Arbëreshe, set up communities in Sicily and continued to use their own language. In fact, standard Italian was Crispi's third language after Albanian and Sicilian. His family had been Orthodox priests and *gabellotti* — that is to say guardians of acreage and property working for the landed gentry. Infamously, some *gabellotti* gained so much power they became proto-*mafiosi*. As Alfio Caruso points out in his book, *I Siciliani* (*The Sicilians*), Crispi came from an area where it was difficult to distinguish between *mafiosi* and non-*mafiosi*.

These ancestral professions were a potent force in forming Crispi's political thought and pugnacious attitudes. Acolytes came to see him at The Palms, where he would hold forth on his political beliefs. He was not so steadfast in his views, however, that his mind could not be changed by events. Once a militant Republican, he declared, post-Risorgimento, that 'the monarchy unites us, a republic would divide us'. Historians see this as the start of his slide from fundamentally democratic principles into the far darker territory of political repression. He was also a master in the art of Machiavellian defamation, denigrating the reputation of opponents — some would say in an attempt to further his own career.

By 1876 Crispi had become President of Italy's Chamber of Deputies and, a year later, he took up the office of Minister of the Interior under Prime Minister Depretis. He had already survived the political machinations of the 1868 Lobbia Affair, something the newspaper *Corriere della Sera* has christened 'Il primo scandalo' — one of many to come in the topsy-turvy world of Italian politics. The affair concerned the giving of a tobacco concession to a company that had never dealt in tobacco. Deputies, in order to vote the concession through, were passed significant bribes. The Republican Giuseppe Ferrari asked for an enquiry into the matter, upon which former Garibaldi campaigner Cristiano

Lobbia stepped forward and brandished two envelopes in Parliament. Realising that an enquiry would not be readily forthcoming, he had decided to draw attention to the evidence he had been collecting about the affair, which included witness statements.

Lobbia set a hare running that caused much panic amongst those who had sold their consciences for money. What did the envelopes actually contain? The intervention had the desired effect and an enquiry could not be avoided. As soon as the commission had been established, newspapers began to attack Lobbia's integrity, and, in an attempt to prevent him from speaking at the enquiry, he was assaulted and injured in the street. Lobbia defended himself in a letter to Crispi's newspaper, *La Riforma*, lamenting the personal attacks on his character and honour. Crispi waded into the argument on behalf of the former *Garibaldino*, hurling violent accusations at those accused of corruption. His indiscriminate allegations probably did more harm than good and he only succeeded in adding fuel to the fire, not to mention calling his own honesty into question.

Lobbia was continuously watched and followed, and eventually was summoned to court on the charge of fabricating a crime against his person. Defence witnesses were intimidated and prosecution witnesses were offered a way out of debt. Ludicrously, as one can see with the benefit of hindsight, Lobbia was sentenced to a year in a military prison. On the occasion of the birth of the future Victor Emmanuel III in 1869, a pardon was granted which Lobbia and his fellow prisoners refused, preferring a retrial which resulted in the overturning of the verdict. Sadly, the clearing of his name was hidden in the back pages of the press and Lobbia never recovered from the opprobrium. Crispi, however, despite his forthright passion, which scared even his followers, survived and flourished.

Whilst in his role as Minister of the Interior, another scandal hit that was far more personal in nature — Crispi was accused of bigamy. His first marriage had lasted only two years before his wife died in childbirth. In 1854 he married Rosalia Montmason, forming a fiery partnership fuelled by her partiality for alcohol and his infidelity. In 1878 Lina Barbagallo came into his life. This daughter of a former Bourbon magistrate captured his heart and his bed — he swiftly married her, but soon found himself in court on charges of bigamy. He escaped the charge on a point of administration; it seemed that his marriage to Montmason in Malta was not conducted by a priest officially sanctioned to carry out marriages and, on his arrival in Sicily, the documentation had not been added to the civil records. Nevertheless, his enemies had enough ammunition to accuse him of immorality and he was forced to resign from political life.

It would be nine years before Crispi could return to high office. In 1887 the old survivor took the top job, becoming Prime Minister, and immediately sparked a trade war with France. He also pursued Italy's belated colonial venture in Ethiopia, a campaign that would prove disastrous for those soldiers caught up in what became known as the Dogali massacre. A troop of 550 men had been sent to reinforce the Italian garrison at Sahati but were surprised at Dogali by an army led by Ras Alula, the Asmara tribal leader. Only eighty men escaped the ensuing slaughter. Crispi described it as 'Italy's Thermopylae' and threatened vengeance. He would not have the opportunity to carry through his threats, however, as the unpopularity of his tax increases and the effects of the trade war with France on agriculture precipitated his resignation.

Like a latter-day Berlusconi, he could not resist one last tilt at power in 1893. This term in office would be his defining moment as Prime Minister as he immediately had to deal with the social unrest stirred up by collectives of workers and peasants known as the *Fasci Siciliani*. The word *fascio* conjures up images of black-shirted militants but although the term (meaning a bundle or binding of sticks) shares a common root with Fascism, the nineteenth-century movement was in fact a left-wing version of early trade unionism. The collectives were campaigning for higher wages, lower taxes, land redistribution and equitable rents — *plus ça change* for the Sicilian peasantry.

The situation rapidly spun out of control when those with vested interests in Sicily's agriculture and mining refused to consider any of the demands. Strikes led to violence and clashes with the police which prompted landowners to ask for government assistance. Crispi declared a state of emergency in January 1894 and despatched 40,000 troops to Sicily. During his own visits he conducted governmental business from The Palms and must have been aware of the degree of repression his actions had instituted. The army rounded up not only the ringleaders, but anyone vaguely connected with the *Fasci*, whether they were students from Palermo, peasants from the interior or merely sympathisers from the professional classes. The ringleaders received lengthy prison sentences and many others were incarcerated for even the most minor offences in a brutal repression that marked the end of the *Fasci* movement.

Crispi had fallen into the trap of believing a conspiracy was behind the *Fasci*, suspecting them to be a front for Sicilian independence financed by his old adversaries the French. In an attempt to assuage the fears of the left, he endeavoured to put through a parliamentary bill appropriating some of the larger estates that could be rented on long leases. Unsurprisingly, the landowners were far from happy. Whilst entangled in this seemingly eternal Sicilian dilemma, the spectre of Ethiopia arose once again with the routing of Italian troops at Adwa in 1896. Crispi resigned and was succeeded by his old nemesis, the Sicilian aristocrat Antonio di Rudinì, the property-owners' candidate.

Rudinì (1839–1908) was of a different stamp to Crispi; he was a marquis who would have employed the likes of Francesco's family to manage his estates. The plush surroundings of The Palms were second nature to such a man, although, rather like Tancredi in *The Leopard*, he supported the *Garibaldini*, perhaps in an attempt to see the sort of change that would keep the status quo. He was not, however, without some liberal credentials, recognising the cruelty of the *Fasci* repressions. Leniency was shown and pardons were issued to a proportion of those who had been summarily thrown in gaol. Throughout his life as a landowner, Rudinì escaped the kind of rebellion seen in Bronte which persuaded the *Encyclopaedia Britannica* to say that 'he managed his estates on liberal lines'. The same publication also called him a '*grand seigneur*', that is to say a non-threatening patrician with old-school manners.

Whilst in his earlier incarnation as the Mayor of Palermo, Rudinì had favoured the arts, announcing competitions for the design and construction of two theatres, the Massimo and Politeama. The contract for the Massimo was won by Giovan Battista Filippo Basile, whose son Ernesto carried on the work after his death and would have a significant impact on The Palms. The burgeoning theatre scene and an explosion in the creative arts attracted a new clientele to Ragusa's hotel. In 1881, not long after the proprietor had launched his journal in homage to the diversity of Sicilian nature, Richard Wagner (1813–83) arrived at The Palms accompanied by his wife, Cosima, and their children, intent on a long stay in the twin hopes of stimulating his creativity and ameliorating his poor health.

Cosima, fortunately for us, was a prolific diarist and we can learn much about his stay through her writing. She was Wagner's second wife, the first being Christine Wilhelmine Planer, known as Minna, who died from a heart condition at the age of fifty-six. Minna and Wagner had a tempestuous marriage during which Wagner had an affair with the German poet and author, Mathilde Wesendonck. It was during his years in Bavaria, under the patronage of Ludwig II, that he met Cosima who, at the time, was married to the conductor Hans von Bülow, who refused to divorce her. It was only after she had given birth to her third child with Wagner that Bülow finally consented. Cosima's father, the composer Franz Lizst, was not happy with the age gap of twenty-four years between his daughter and Wagner or the scandal that the affair created in Munich, although the pair remained friends and Lizst was in attendance at some of Wagner's greatest triumphs.

Simon Callow, in his book *Being Wagner: The Triumph of the Will*, paints an evocative portrait of the composer at the height of his powers, just five years before he travelled to Palermo. The scene is the Festspielhaus in Bayreuth at the premiere of *The Twilight of the Gods*. The audience contained not only Lizst, but Bruckner, Grieg, Rubenstein and Tchaikovsky, as well as a sprinkling of the crowned heads of Europe and lesser aristocracy. At the end of the performance, the concert hall erupted into a crescendo of appreciation and a tiny figure shuffled to the centre of the stage to take the applause. Callow tells us that Tchaikovsky thought Wagner looked every inch and more of his sixty-three years, a fragile, hunched man, seemingly incapable of a work of such magnitude.

In 1881 Wagner's doctor fetched a specialist from the university town of Erlangen to fully assess the maestro's health. Having ascertained that all seemed in working order, the specialist pronounced a strict dietary regime and sunshine. Initially, the Wagner family headed for Naples and were dazzled by the luminosity, both during the day and at night.

On the boat trip to Palermo, as the composer noted in a letter to Ludwig II, the moonlight was 'glorious'. They arrived in the city on 5 November to brilliant sunshine. In the same letter, Wagner tells the king that they had taken rooms in The Palms, where he was clearly entranced by the gardens and felt sure that he would regain his health in such an environment. Cosima, in her diary, details that they were given rooms 24, 25 and 26 which afforded them a view of the gardens from the conservatory terrace.

Their first trip around Palermo proved something of a disappointment in comparison to Naples, an opinion that was soon to change. The blousy charms of the Vesuvian city presented themselves immediately; Palermo's attraction, however, as many other visitors have also found, required more coaxing. Within days Cosima wrote that they 'spent a long time in the evening sitting on the terrace (conservatory) in moonlight. The idyllic aspect of Palermo is beginning to captivate us.' In addition to the delights of the terrace, Wagner was happy with the rooms and began to organise his workspace in the salon. A sepia-tinted photograph of the interior exists showing an ornate chandelier above a central table; a gilded mirror dominates the wall above the fireplace and swagged curtains add a homely feel to what could otherwise seem rather grandiose.

It was in these surroundings that Wagner set to work on completing *Parsifal*, an opera whose libretto he had begun in 1865. The work is Wagner's take on the Grail legend in which a wounded Amfortas, the keeper of the Grail, reveals the holy vessel to Parsifal. A mysterious woman called Kundry, condemned to perpetual penance for mocking Christ, lures Parsifal to Klingsor's magic castle where the young man rejects her advances and is cursed to wander aimlessly. Klingsor now appears and throws a sacred spear at Parsifal who catches it and, by making the sign of the cross, destroys Klingsor's fortress. In the final act, years later, the eldest Knight of the Grail, Gurnemanz, comes across an ailing Kundry and revives her with holy water; then spies a knight in black armour with a spear who turns out to be none other than Parsifal. Parsifal is then crowned King of the Grail and, using the spear, heals Amfortas' eternal wound. Finally, he lifts the Grail to the accompaniment of a white dove. At this, Kundry falls to the ground with her life draining away.

Musicologists and historians find *Parsifal* one of Wagner's most problematic works. In conjunction with the completion of the opera, Wagner published an essay called 'Heroism and Christianity' in which he gave free reign to the most bizarre and objectionable of his opinions. He proposed the insidious and unconscionable belief that the Aryans, his 'German leaders of mankind', were descendants of the Gods and that everyone else had derived from Darwin's apes. In creating the character Parsifal, he is proclaiming an Aryan Christ rather than the Jewish originator of Christianity. The paradox that confronts many drawn to Wagner's work is that the music, language and choreography form a perfect synergy, a harmony never previously achieved. The first performance of the opera was conducted by Hermann Levi who Wagner tried to coerce into baptism because he did not want to hand over the score to a Jew. Quite rightly, Levi refused although he continued in his role. The philosopher Nietzsche, who had previously been an admirer of Wagner, was appalled by the opera and called it 'a work of malice, of vindictiveness ... an outrage on morality'.

Cosima's informal journal is full of references to her husband's composition and, at various intervals, she mentions that he would run through a segment of music with her, looking for feedback and reassurance that he had achieved his intended aim. Cosima was a woman of musical understanding given her family credentials, but she seldom contradicted his feelings with regard to the direction of his work. They were clearly compatible and during their stay in Palermo Wagner once wistfully commented that he regretted the fact that they had not discovered each other ten or fifteen years earlier. Cosima, for her part, felt that all the beauty surrounding them in the city would mean nothing without him.

They did not restrict themselves to strolls through the city streets and gardens, and occasionally ventured further afield into the Conca d'Oro, the bowl-shaped hinterland behind Palermo dotted with orange and lemon groves. Their first excursion was to the Cathedral of Monreale. Surprisingly, Cosima makes no specific mention of the gold mosaics that cover the interior of the building. There are 130 scenes depicting biblical and other religious events, and a plethora of figures which amount to 10,000 square metres of tesserae, making it one of the most of heavily-mosaicked buildings in the world. Work on the structure began in 1174 after it was commissioned by the Norman king William II, who was heavily advised in the choice of iconography by his clergy, some of whom had connections with that other Norman outpost, England.

Although the overall impression on the Wagners was one of sublimity, they were most enchanted by the cloisters which flank the south side of the Cathedral. The Romanesque design is a perfect square with the arcading supported by a sequence of double pillars decorated with a variety of patterns made from inlaid mosaic and lava stone. It was William II's idea to introduce the oriental element of water by adding a corner fountain which is also housed in a miniature cloister with barley-sugar columns topped by ornate terracotta tiling. The area is a perfect place to escape the heat and to dream.

The Wagners avoided the excesses of a Sicilian summer, but were occasionally plagued by two debilitating elements of these southern latitudes — irritating mosquitoes and the enervating wind known as the Sirocco which blows in directly from the Sahara. The wind is infamous for its ability to sap strength and alter the mood of anyone attempting to achieve a task involving either thought or physical effort. The greatest mood enhancer for Cosima and Richard was Shakespeare and they would spend most evenings reading aloud from one of his plays. After visiting Monreale, they decided that 'nothing less than Shakespeare will do' and they settled down to read *Henry VI, Part I*. According to Cosima, Wagner exclaimed: 'He is the greatest of them all — What images!'

Wagner clearly appreciated and employed a high degree of visual acuity, enabling him to conjure Shakespeare's characters in his mind's eye as if they were players in one of his own operas. *Henry VI* was perfect for the composer in that it covers a stormy period of English history which saw a high-stakes game for political power. The play begins in 1422 as the Duke of Gloucester has been appointed Lord Protector during the infancy of Henry VI, although the Bishop of Winchester fears he is trying to usurp power. Meanwhile in France the English are besieging Orléans in a bid to drive out the French. As this battle rages, the rival factions at home ask their followers to pick red or white roses to show their allegiance; this will ultimately result in the civil war known as the Wars of the Roses. Joan la Pucelle, otherwise known as Joan of Arc, disguises

herself as she leads the French to retake Rouen and is involved in a plot
to persuade the Duke of Burgundy to change sides. The play ends with
Richard Plantagenet, Duke of York, condemning Joan of Arc to death
and Henry VI accepting the hand of Margaret of Anjou. The synopsis
reads like a super-charged Machiavellian fight for dominance. It is easy
to imagine Wagner, with play in hand, strutting over the carpeted floor
of the salon and giving full force to the Duke of Exeter's simile: 'Like
captives bound to a triumphant car.'

Wagner's Shakespearean obsession even extended to nicknaming
Via Maqueda, the thoroughfare that crosses Via Vittorio Emanuele at
the Quattro Canti. His play on words morphed the already Hispanic
Maqueda into Macbetha. The greatest talent he saw in Shakespeare was
his ability to bring characters to life in an authentic manner as 'living
beings'. It was a gift he also recognised in the Bard's great Spanish
contemporary, Cervantes. Wagner may not have realised, but the author
of Don Quixote knew Sicily well. During his time as a soldier, Cervantes
recovered from the Battle of Lepanto at a hospital in Messina, the city
with which he was most familiar, but he also knew Palermo and Trapani
from when the Spanish fleet docked at both ports.

The Wagners would have these literary discussions whilst walking
through Palermo's gardens, either those attached to villas, or more
public spaces such as the Giardino Inglese. It is once again the Basile
family, specifically Giovan Battista Filippo, that we have to thank for
this approximation of an English garden in the heart of the city. His
intention was to move away from the strict, geometric formality of an
Italian garden, creating a more natural feel in tune with the environment
and terrain. He planted a bosco, a woodland that may have been English
in concept but is much more in sympathy with the climate. Today, there
are many exotic species amongst which are the Canary Island Dragon
Tree, the Illawarra flame tree from Australia and another antipodean
species, the Moreton Bay fig, a further example of which also famously
fills Palermo's Piazza Marina.

Giovan Battista Filippo's son, Ernesto, added a little pavilion in
Arab-Norman style with a crenelated roof surround, underscored by
a geometrically patterned panel that also outlines the arched doorway
and grilled windows. The effect of the diminutive folly in the middle of

the glade, simulating the hunting lodge of a medieval Norman king, has been somewhat lost by the addition of an expanse of concrete poured over what would once have been earth and gravel. Basile took his inspiration from the ruined palazzo known as La Cuba and the Castello della Zisa, two remnants of the Normans' obsessional embrace of Saracen culture.

Both buildings are beyond the Porta Nuova which signals the start of the Via Vittorio Emanuele. Of the two, the Zisa is in a better state of repair. The structure was started in the twelfth century by Arab craftsmen employed by William I and was intended as a summer residence for the Norman kings. There are echoes of the great Moorish buildings of Spain in the honeycomb carvings of the niches and the term *al-Aziz* (splendid) etched above the entrance in Arabic script. When Wagner first visited in December 1881, he was in the company of Count Giuseppe Tasca Lanza, which was probably a wise move in terms of gaining the appropriate introductions as the Zisa was then owned by the powerful Notarbartolo family who can trace their lineage through the upheavals of European conflict right back to the fifth-century lords of Alsace.

Tasca took Wagner in his carriage, thereby saving his aristocratic legs and avoiding the onset of his ailing guest's heart palpitations. The Wagners were soon receiving Tasca at the hotel and visiting the Count at his villa along what is now known as Viale della Regione Siciliana. Originally constructed in the 1500s, it featured one of Palermo's most sumptuous Victorian-style gardens, complete with winding pathways through luxurious lawns surrounded by tropical vegetation. Today, the pale honey-coloured palazzo can be hired for auspicious occasions. Just before World War I, the Romanian-French writer Anna de Noailles was so beguiled by the villa that she described it as a location which finally enabled her to appreciate 'the full beauty, the noble and peaceful splendour, of Palermo's pure and immense light'. Wagner thought the villa 'magnificent' and noted the interior design that reflected the antiquity of Ancient Rome. One room is frescoed in such a manner that the visitor could almost walk through the *trompe l'oeil* archways as they romantically crumble to reveal the supposed landscape and statuary beyond.

Giuseppe Tasca (1849–1917) is the first Sicilian to be regularly mentioned in Cosima's diaries. He had studied chemistry at Palermo

University and used this to inform the cultivation of his land, employing the most up-to-date technological advancements in the whole of the Conca d'Oro. At the turn of the century, twenty years after Wagner had left Sicily, he would become the Mayor of Palermo — a move into politics that inspired his son, Lucio, who was one of the leading instigators in the move towards Sicilian independence after the Allies' invasion, as we shall see in chapter 4.

The terrace, conservatory and gardens of The Palms made a perfect venue for receiving Tasca. Cosima always found him friendly and was delighted to discover that his wife knew German. In addition to discussing the merits of places the couple should visit during their stay, the conversation occasionally turned to the wider world. Unfortunately, the detail of such conversations is not recorded by Cosima, but we have other glimpses into her own discussions with Wagner. During coffee after one memorable lunch, the topics ranged from Wagner's loathing of Rococo design to his thoughts on Nietzsche, whose ideas he had grown to hate. Later, he made the family laugh with a caricature of the modern world as he saw it — prancing horses, a noble, hardworking coachman and a 'bloated Jewish banker' inside the coach. When pressed to give strong opinions, his prejudices would seemingly always rise to the surface. He knew Jewish musicians and bankers who were gentiles, but the caricature overruled the reality.

Throughout the diary, however, Cosima shows us Wagner's compassion for the poverty he saw around him in Palermo. In response to Sicilians listing the progress being made in society, he would always issue a retort about the state of begging on the island. During their stay, he and Cosima noticed, with sadness, a young woman holding her baby and picking through the rubbish. There was also a beggar who habitually propped up the doorpost opposite their hotel room, using the scant shelter this provided in order to escape the biting winter wind. The couple would watch him struggle to obtain alms from anyone other than the occasional passing tourist. Despite this, Wagner reserved an even greater sympathy for the animal world. When walking home via the Teatro Politeama, he saw a boy mistreating his dog. In an exasperated rage, the composer berated him in pigeon Italian that went unheeded, largely thanks to Wagner's lack of vocabulary and execrable accent.

The encounter was enough to persuade him to learn Italian, simply for the purpose of rescuing a tormented puppy.

The hotel's terrace was a playground for two monkeys that amused the Wagner family with their antics. The composer was fond of trying to playfully tap the unsuspecting simians and, on one occasion, his game was anticipated by the more astute monkey, who turned and smacked him before he was able to approach. The memory of this spectacle was spoilt for evermore when Richard discovered that one of the monkeys had died by feasting on a cactus offered by a naïve boy, and the remaining primate could be seen mourning the loss of its friend. Wagner's response was to suggest that little else could be expected from a creature who went around walking upright on two legs. The terrace subsequently fell out of favour, forever tainted.

The Wagners were delighted to hear that the hotel proprietor was a butterfly specialist. Ragusa occasionally visited his illustrious clients to ensure that all was to their satisfaction. In his perfect German he would enquire after the maestro's health and ask if any adjustments were required to the rooms or the food. Sometimes this merely consisted of a few sentences and a nod of assurance; at other times the conversation would broaden to diverse matters. On 12 December 1881, Cosima records how Ragusa told them of his entomological passion and shocked the couple by revealing the carelessness of butterfly collecting. The fashion for pinning these delicate, brightly coloured insects to boards for display in glass cabinets had led to the decimation of entire species. Ragusa must have been aware that he was not entirely without blame himself, but he did at least restrict his collections in an attempt to prevent such loss.

Although Ragusa was keen to facilitate a comfortable stay, it clearly had a price tag. Consequently, Wagner was always rather circumspect in the company of the man he referred to as his 'landlord'. This was not so with more intimate friends, notably the composer Anton Rubenstein who was waiting to greet the Wagners when they first arrived in Palermo. On one occasion Rubenstein was playing a Beethoven sonata and this triggered a conversation on the comparison between painting and music. Wagner could not understand how anyone could compare Mozart's compositions with Raphael's artwork, tacitly realising that his own musical imagery would find little comparison in more physical manifestations. It was with this mindset that he received the Impressionist painter, Pierre-Auguste Renoir, who had his own unique way of expressing the reality he perceived.

Renoir (1876–1919), a leader in the Impressionist movement, had been trying to earn a living through portrait commissions, as can be seen from his submissions to the second Impressionist exhibition in 1876. Following this, he extended his range of subject matter for the third exhibition, which included his now famous canvas, *Dance at Le Moulin de la Galette*. The painting that sealed his fame was that of *Mme Charpentier and her Children*. The lady in question, wearing a long black dress edged in white lace, is relaxing on a chaise with her two young daughters, one of whom has her legs draped over the family dog. The picture exudes luxury and privilege, but also warmth and affection. Madame Charpentier and her husband, Georges, were significant art collectors and she was one of the earliest champions of Impressionist art.

It was Georges Charpentier (1846–1905) who gave Renoir the commission to paint the portrait of Wagner. By 1880, Renoir had decided that a degree of travelling would broaden his painterly horizons. Initially he travelled to Algeria in the footsteps of Eugène Delacroix who had painted over one hundred scenes of everyday life in North Africa. From the souks of Tangier he travelled to Madrid in order to study the art of Diego Velázquez, perhaps the greatest of all the Spanish Golden Age painters. Any tour in search of artistic inspiration would not be complete without seeing the Italian masters however; with this in mind, Renoir headed over the Alps to Italy. He spent two months in the country, making his way through the peninsula, taking in the delights of masterpieces by Titian and Raphael along the way. He was particularly struck by Raphael's frescos in the Villa Farnesina, lamenting that he had not put them at the top of his agenda. He described them in a letter to the art dealer Paul Durand-Ruel as being 'full of knowledge and wisdom'.

As Renoir made his way to Palermo, Wagner was putting the finishing touches to *Parsifal*. Surprisingly, the Frenchman had struggled, thus far, to persuade Italians to pose for him. He had managed to paint the head of a woman in Venice and a mother and child in Naples, but the problem he encountered was his inability to chat in a friendly manner with the locals, having no knowledge of Italian. He was to find that he would have little time for idle chit-chat with the German maestro during the portrait session itself, although he did manage a conversation with Wagner in the hotel bar during the previous day. Cosima says that the sitting was scheduled for 12 o'clock prompt in his suite at The Palms on Sunday 15 January 1882. In Barbara Ehrlich White's biography of the painter she says that the session lasted a mere thirty-five minutes.

Wagner was amused by the fact that he had initially mistaken Renoir for the French journalist Victor Noir, as both sported facial hair and wavy locks. As the Frenchman worked in a frenzy on the portrait, his excitability and facial grimaces added to the composer's amusement. The result, with its delicate use of a blue background and pink tones on the face, caused Wagner to say that it made him look like 'the embryo of an angel, an oyster swallowed by an epicure'. Following the sitting, Renoir put pen to paper to tell Charpentier that, if he liked the image, he could inscribe it with a wording that detailed the date, location and the fact that it had been painted the day after Wagner had completed *Parsifal*. As Ehrlich White notes, he added that he was uncontrollably nervous during the painting of the commission and had wished that he was Jean-Auguste-Dominique Ingres — his predecessor and a man who had painted many prestigious portraits. Renoir blamed his nerves on pushing his shyness to the limit.

Incredibly, Renoir also thought that the final result would have been better if he had stopped sooner, given that the initial good humour displayed by the composer had soon been replaced by a certain stiffness of manner. Renoir felt that he had allowed his brush to follow this change in demeanour too closely. Perhaps this led to Wagner's famous repost: 'Ah! Ah! It's true that I look like a Protestant minister.' While it is true to say that there is something of the Presbyterian minister about his countenance with its white whiskered jawline, the overall effect is of an artistic man capable of deep thought, but seemingly intransigent if challenged and rather haughty in his dealings with the wider world.

The portrait's future fared better than that of Georges Charpentier himself. The man who had commissioned Renoir was soon to see the fortunes of his publishing company go from bad to worse. Matters did not improve when he launched an illustrated newspaper called *La Vie moderne*, even though he had Renoir as an associate illustrator. Charpentier took on extra investors but to no avail as authors moved to other publications and the number of releases dwindled. The Charpentiers were forced to sell some of their precious art collection. The portrait of Wagner eventually ended up in the Musée d'Orsay in Paris, where art critics, notably Julius Meier-Graefe, tell us that the hastily completed 'little souvenir' reveals aspects of Wagner with an 'astonishing, almost pitiless, psychology'. As a footnote, Renoir produced a graphite and charcoal copy of the work for Charpentier's *La Vie moderne* to accompany the paper's obituary of the composer on his death in 1883.

Wagner was happier in the company of those less likely to scrutinise his every thought and movement, particularly those with musical leanings. It was almost inevitable that Tina Scalia would be dragged into his orbit. Tina (1858–1957) was the daughter of General Alfonso Scalia, who had been part of Garibaldi's campaign. Prior to the Risorgimento the family had been exiled in London, where Tina was born. In the years following unification, Alfonso was posted to various parts of Italy and the family eventually found their way back to Palermo. His daughter's recollections of first setting foot in the city at that time are associated with the black drapes displayed for the mourning of Ben Ingham, whose death would eventually lead to the sale of Palazzo Ingham to Enrico Ragusa.

Tina had been trained as a singer and had taken lessons from the soprano Virginia Boccabadati in Turin, and from the baritone Ferlotti in Bologna, both of whom were famous in their day. The family held hopes that their prodigy would one day make an appearance at La Scala in Milan. Tina had made friends with Lily Belmonte, the daughter of the Prince of Pandolfina, whose family owned a villa below Monte Pellegrino, and it was through Lily that Tina met various aristocrats from German and Russian nobility including the Grand Duchess Vladimir. She was occasionally called to sing at soirées but, sadly, her musical career stalled and her interest remained nothing more than a hobby.

Tina was also increasingly spending time with the Whitakers and had caught the eye of Joseph Whitaker, who was the son of Joseph (Benjamin Ingham Senior's nephew) and known to all as Pip. Initially, Pip had been more interested in a certain Alice Bennett but had eventually succumbed to Tina's charms. The moment of connection was distinctly lacking in fireworks; Raleigh Trevelyan, quoting Tina, says that Pip was simply taken by the fact that his dogs repeatedly trailed after her and so, trusting in their canine instinct, decided that she was the one for him.

It was during their courtship that Tina Scalia was summoned to The Palms in order to meet Wagner. Her recollections are anything but sympathetic. She found him conceited, overbearing and totally wrapped up in his own thoughts to the extent that he ignored those around him. Cosima's devotion to her husband did not help matters, especially when the muse struck. Tina recalls one occasion when the maestro stopped mid-sentence and looked off into the far distance as though thunderstruck. Cosima was keen that everybody should know he had been overcome by 'an inspiration' and asked people to leave lest the spell be broken. This conjures the image of a pompous Wagner, dismissing mere mortals who could possibly taint his genius. Tina goes on to say that during such an inspiration, Cosima would throw a coloured veil over his head to exclude the outside world and encourage his visions.

It was at a celebration given by Count Tasca that Tina was able to demonstrate her singing prowess in front of the composer. She sang items from his early repertoire and also an aria from *Lohengrin*. Tina was embarrassed when an ecstatic Wagner demonstrably demanded encores before the rest of the audience had begun their appreciation. It was not the only time she sang for him. During a run-through of some extracts from *Parsifal* in the presence of Prince Constantine of Russia, Wagner asked for a third repetition of a particular passage he had liked. This was too much for the Prince, who hastily took his leave, saluting as he went.

Tina is one of the few to verify Cosima's assertion that Wagner found The Palms increasingly expensive. On 23 January 1882, Wagner and Cosima took a carriage to Bagheria with a view to renting a villa called the Casa Ferdinande; this was not the first time they had investigated alternative accommodation. On the same day, their friend Tasca arrived with Prince Gangi who was prepared to rent them his villa in the countryside surrounding Palermo. After a perusal of the building and its grounds, they happily accepted the Prince's offer and the family gave notice to the hotel. Wagner is reputed to have held the sentiment that the biggest thief on the island was The Palms' proprietor.

The following day saw the family make preparations to leave. Wagner received a communiqué from Ragusa but sadly Cosima makes no reference to the contents except to say that 'all is settled peacefully, R. as usual prepared to make payment in full'. It is left to Tina to tell us that Ragusa had been annoyed by the fact that the composer and his family had booked to stay for several months and were leaving earlier than expected; consequently, Ragusa demanded a degree of compensation for this loss of income. Without further evidence to the contrary, we have to assume that a conciliatory amount was paid in order to leave in the peaceful manner described by Cosima. We do not know if the wider Wagnerian circle, including the artist Joukowski and the composer Rubenstein, left at the same time.

Coincidentally, Tina was involved in matchmaking for Blandine von Bülow, Cosima's daughter from her first marriage, although it was Tasca who eventually introduced Blandine to Count Biagio Gravina, who had fallen on financial hard times but came from the same prestigious family as the Prince from Bagheria whose Villa Palagonia was adorned with monsters. The couple went on to marry and Wagner was able to attend the engagement in Acireale, where he came face to face with Garibaldi shortly before the leader's death. Not long after the celebration, the Wagner family left the island and took up residence in Venice where the composer died in February 1883. In the same year Pip and Tina were married, forming a partnership that would be at the heart of Palermitan social circles for years to come, with the shy, retiring Pip leaving the entertaining to his more outgoing wife. Interestingly, the wedding reception took place in the Hotel Trinacria and not The Palms.

The traces left behind by Wagner were strong enough to pass into legend, and tales of him reached the ears of Guy de Maupassant (1850–93). After the publication of *Bel-Ami* in 1885, the author and his friends Amic, Legrand and Gervex toured Italy. Having visited Venice and Rome Maupassant, especially, was drawn to Sicily. The writer starts his account of the trip, published in *La Vie Errante*, with this lament regarding the island's relative lack of visitors:

The French are under the impression that Sicily is a wild country, difficult of access, and even dangerous to explore. Now and then some traveler [sic], who is thought very daring, ventures as far as Palermo, and returns with the information that it is a very interesting town. But what makes Palermo and all Sicily so interesting? No one can tell. To tell the truth, this is only a question of custom. This island, a jewel of the Mediterranean, is not on the list of those countries usually visited by tourists ... From two special points of view, however, Sicily should attract travelers [sic], because its natural and artistic beauties are as singular as they are wonderful.

Stepping from the boat, Maupassant was immediately struck by the bustling shops and commercial animation of the people. It was a time when those involved in economic activity still transported goods using the famous Sicilian cart, now consigned to museums and exhibitions of traditional folk life. The Frenchman marvelled at the brightly hand-painted waggons with their 'crude and odd paintings, representing historical facts, adventures of all kinds'. If he found the carts naively attractive, he was transported to another realm by the Palatine Chapel inside the Palazzo dei Normanni. Roger II commissioned this masterwork of Byzantine gold mosaic, Arab-style wood carving and inlaid tilework in the twelfth century. Maupassant's awed prose encapsulates the radiance: 'The calm beauty and attractiveness of this little chapel, which is positively the most wonderful masterpiece of its kind, causes one to stand entranced before these walls ... shining with a soft light that dimly illuminates the whole edifice, leading one's mind into biblical and heavenly landscapes ...'

In a state of almost meditative bliss, Maupassant leisurely made his way to The Palms, where his serene state of mind leads him to pick up the story thus:

I came back slowly to the Hotel of the Palms, which has one of the finest gardens in the city, — the gardens of tropical countries, filled with enormous and strange plants. A traveler [sic], seated on a bench, gives me in a few words the events of the past year, and going back to the memories of by-gone years, he says, among other things: 'This happened when Wagner lived here.' Astonished at this, I said: 'What, here, in this hotel?' 'Why, yes, it was while here that he wrote the last notes of "Parsifal" and corrected the proofs.'

Maupassant, on further enquiry, realised that Wagner had left a strong impression of his immutability which corresponds remarkably with Tina Scalia's account. Maupassant noted the maestro's reckless temper, insufferable arrogance and disdain for company; nevertheless he was most keen to go in search of the hotel room occupied by the German, and swiftly sought out Ragusa, requesting that the proprietor show him Wagner's suite. Ragusa was only too happy to oblige and took him to the desired location where Maupassant proceeded to look for an object, a chair, a table, anything that contained the essence of the man. Ragusa pointed out the couch that Wagner had requested and explained that the maestro had covered it with rugs worked in gold thread.

Just as Maupassant was conjuring an image of the recumbent composer, he found an even more evocative object:

> Then I opened the door of a mirrored cabinet. A delicious and powerful perfume blew out, like the caress of a breeze passing over a field of roses. The owner of the place, who was my guide, said: 'He kept his clothes in here, after perfuming them with the essence of roses. This odor [sic] will never evaporate.' I inhaled this breath of flowers, inclosed [sic] in this piece of furniture, forgotten here, a captive; and it seemed, in truth, as if I had found something of Wagner, in this perfume which he loved — a little of his personality, of his desires, of his soul, in this mere trifle, of the secret and beloved habits which are the making of the intimate life of a man.

Raleigh Trevelyan highlights Tina's claim that the veil thrown over Wagner in moments of inspiration was designed to produce 'roseate' ideas. However, Trevelyan then brings us all down to earth by explaining that Wagner's overuse of rose perfume was due to the fact that he had a reduced sense of smell caused by his liberal intake of snuff.

If Maupassant let his imagination fly with these olfactory reminiscences of Wagner, his subsequent descriptions of the Sicilian in the street are far more rooted in close observation. He found nothing of the Neapolitan in the average Palermitan, but was impressed with a sedateness of manner that he attributed to an Arab influence. He also felt that Sicilians more resembled Spaniards than Italians, both in terms of facial features and native pride. The only place where he felt that a Sicilian became thoroughly Italianised was at the opera, something which, no doubt, would have pleased and horrified Wagner:

> Every impression of the public is expressed as soon as felt. Excessively nervous, gifted with an ear as true as it is sensitive, loving music to distraction, the entire audience becomes a sort of vibrating animal, which feels but cannot reason. In five minutes it will applaud an actor with enthusiasm and hiss him with frenzy; it stamps with joy or with rage, and if a false note falls from the throat of a singer, a strange cry, exasperated and in a high key, bursts from every voice at the same time.

Being the popular refrains of the day, opera arias were hummed in the streets by the populace and Maupassant was amused to hear Bizet's *Carmen*, specifically the 'Toreador Song', on the lips of the city's inhabitants.

As captivated as he was by Palermo, the capital could not hold him forever. His first venture inland was to Monreale and its cathedral, William II's masterpiece of mosaic art. From the town, he scanned the surrounding mountains and spotted a ruined fortress on one of the summits which, according to a local inhabitant, was the ultimate redoubt of those involved in brigandage. He was warned off approaching the citadel, known as Castellaccio, for the obvious reason, but also because the path was deemed difficult and treacherous. Obstinately, he insisted on going and had to resort to a guide recommended by the Chief of Police.

Unfortunately, the guide turned out to be clueless and asked every passer-by for directions. The climb became tortuous and the party had to scramble over rocks underneath a burning sun before they reached the tumbledown castle with its 'chaos of enormous gray [sic] stones'. Maupassant was rewarded with a stunning view of Palermo and its necklace of orange trees looping around the Conca d'Oro. His climb was considered ill-advised and certainly not an excursion to be recommended to a woman.

Female travellers attempting to break out of these shackles were few and far between in this era of conservative Victorianism. A notable exception was Margaret Fountaine (1862–1940), the daughter of an Anglican vicar from South Acre in East Anglia who, despite her quiet provincial upbringing, managed to fulfil her longing to experience the wider world. She travelled alone in her pursuit of butterflies, a passion that would lead to renown in the field of lepidopterology. In 1896 she set off for Sicily, and arrived at The Palms with two aims in mind — one was to base herself in comfortable surroundings, and the other was to meet Enrico Ragusa who, as we know, was a man after her own heart.

Many years later, when Fountaine died at the age of seventy-seven, her extensive butterfly collection was bequeathed to the Castle Museum at Norwich with the curious codicil that the boxes should not be opened until 1978, some thirty-eight years after her death. The mystery as to why these collections could not see the light of day for such a long period of time was solved when the lid was removed from one unprepossessing container. Inside were a dozen cloth-bound diaries, revealing more than mere scientific procedure. Interwoven with the accounts of her beloved butterflies were far more gossipy pages detailing, with surprising candour for the era, her romantic liaisons. This rare opportunity to gaze into the inner world of an adventurous woman with the veil of propriety removed proved too tempting for W.F. Carter, the assistant editor of the *Sunday Times*, who edited the diaries into two volumes.

Published as *Love Among the Butterflies* (1980) and *Butterflies and Late Loves* (1986), the diaries inevitably attracted attention for reasons other than lepidopterological study. The first volume is subtitled 'The diaries of a wayward, determined and passionate Victorian lady'. The description on the back cover details the litany of men who fell for Fountaine's charms, including an Egyptian mariner, a Hungarian noble, a Syrian dragoman and a Sicilian butterfly hunter. The hunter in question was not Signor Ragusa; however, as she tells us in her diary, she wasted no time in contacting The Palms' proprietor, who was able to provide her with much useful information concerning the species she was interested in finding, specifically *M. Pherusa*. She points out that this genus had very specific localities and only a man of Ragusa's knowledge could direct her to its actual habitat on Monte Cuccio, approximately eight kilometres from Palermo.

The intrepid Fountaine was only too happy to scrabble over the rocks of Monte Cuccio, net in hand, heedless of the loose terrain, weather and spiky vegetation. Her tenacity was rewarded with the specimens she craved which she would pin out in display boxes once back in her room. Fountaine gives us a wonderful evocation of the attention she attracted when walking through central Palermo in her field attire, complete with a knapsack. Everyone from sellers of sponges to carriage drivers and beggars would approach her for custom, money or more nefarious reasons. On one occasion, three dandified youths engaged her in conversation. The expected reaction of a lone Victorian woman would be one of polite coldness and a hasty retreat. Instead, she agreed to accompany them for the morning — even taking an excursion to the church of Santa Maria di Jesu along dusty roads in order to admire the view.

After stopping for a drink of lemon water with the young men, a fourth youth joined the party and took a particular interest in Fountaine. Against her better judgement, she found herself accepting an offer to attend the theatre with them that evening. Back at the hotel, she fell in with a bearded Italian who lent her his Baedeker guide. Still uncertain as to whether she had been rash in accepting the theatre proposal, she asked her new friend for advice. He casually told her to attend if she was interested in the performance, but suggested that she spend the evening with him instead. As it turned out, there was no performance that night but Fountaine agreed to a walk with one of the youths along the Marina, although as she records, she 'soon saw the bent of his inclinations'. Eventually, the young man made the comical proposition that he would like to come up to see her butterflies. Realising exactly what that meant, she parried with the suggestion that she could bring the collection down to the public salon for him to see. She never saw him again.

Meanwhile, the bearded Italian was less easily dissuaded and managed to convince Fountaine to accompany him on a trip to Villa Belmonte, where the couple rambled through the mix of cultivation and chaos found in the villa's grounds. The gentleman turned out to be a baron and apparently behaved impeccably during the many hours the pair spent together. Not all of Fountaine's male admirers were so highly-born. In Taormina, she was wooed by the son of a hotel keeper who flooded her with compliments in their mutually-understood French and, in Messina, a fellow tourist propositioned her on the way back to her room and later knocked on her door, just in case she had changed her mind.

Relieved to have rebuffed these advances, she was much happier in the company of young Signor Amenta who assisted her collecting and shared her interest. They roamed the landscape in search of the species *Charaxes Iasius* and she calls her partner in crime the 'dark-eyed youth'. They took picnics with them which they ate under the benign branches of an olive tree, seemingly wrapped up in the splendid surroundings and each other's company. She found Amenta both attractive and amenable, but is at pains to point out that their relationship was platonic.

During one memorable excursion to Monte Ciccia, they found a species whose identity they could not agree upon. Fountaine decided she would take it back to Ragusa for discussion and possible identification. Ragusa was thrilled to find that the butterfly in question was completely new to Sicily and therefore he carefully packaged it and sent it on to a German expert who might be able to verify its name. Back in Palermo, Fountaine also renewed her friendship with the baron who had now decided to cut to the chase and lay bare his intentions. Tired of being a powerless woman and constantly rejecting advances, she came to the startlingly modern conclusion, under the baron's influence, that free love was better than wedlock, believing that married couples soon became tired of each other — a state which would lead to shameful infidelity. She considered convention to be more easily broken when unmarried. This new perspective led to a tentative tumble in the brushwood with Amenta but she only went so far, realising that, despite his looks and their mutual lepidopterist passion, love was missing.

Fountaine's diary also makes reference to an unnamed professor, whom she had presumably met in Sicily for lepidopterological reasons. She agreed to yet another evening stroll during which the professor suggested, rather rashly, that they run into the sea together. They had intended to visit some gardens, although she neglects to reveal which of Palermo's green spaces they had decided upon. Instead, the devious academic led her along some very dark and twisting alleyways where he suddenly produced handkerchiefs for them to sit on and suggested they pause for a while. 'Here we go again' could not have been far from her mind and she tells us that kissing a man to whom she was indifferent was not an experience to be repeated. She went back to the hotel for a much-needed wash — neck, eyes, ears and face. Not to tar everyone with the same brush, she later realised that, far from making an improper proposition, the professor had intended to ask for her hand in marriage. Needless to say, this was not on her agenda and the mere thought of tying the knot with such a grizzled older man repelled Fountaine.

Aside from promoting a change in her philosophy to life, Sicily also provided the catalyst for her scientific career. In the year following the trip, at the age of twenty-seven, she saw her first paper published in *The Entomologist's Record and Journal of Variation*. Her ramblings with Amenta had not been in vain; she was able to detail for her article both the habitats and butterfly species to be found in Sicily. In the same year, a considerable inheritance left to Fountaine and her sisters by their uncle afforded her even greater independence, and facilitated a lifetime of travel from Budapest to Baalbek and the Sea of Galilee to Sikkim.

Sadly, we do not know if Ragusa wrote to inform Fountaine of the Monte Ciccia butterfly's identity or, indeed, if his German expert had even been able to provide enlightenment. Ragusa would have delighted in finding someone equally enthusiastic about the science of lepidopterology. However, he was increasingly reminded that his real love was not the means by which he sustained his family and status. The Palms was a constant nagging presence that required attention.

Elsewhere in Palermo, Tina Whitaker continued to invite guests to stay who had originally intended to spend a period of time at the hotel. Pip and Tina had commissioned a villa to be built in Via Dante, just a thirty-minute walk from The Palms. Tina now held court at the Villa Malfitano, where visitors would gather in the *sala d'estate* (summer room) with its delicately painted frescoes mimicking the iron-strutted frames of a glasshouse through which are depicted the kind of lush vegetation to be found in the gardens of Ragusa's hotel — palms, trailing vines, bright Mediterranean flowers standing tall through the undergrowth — all against the soft blue and wispy cloud of an early morning sky. Mr and Mrs Whitaker were moving in exulted circles; Pip thought nothing of rubbing shoulders with people of illustrious lineage including Luigi Medici, who casually gifted Whitaker some red deer for the Malfitano estate. Those travelling from Britain often arrived proffering a letter from a mutual acquaintance who could assure the Whitakers of their good standing even if, in reality, they had a raffish reputation.

Some of the aristocracy who pitched up at Tina's door carried considerable metaphorical baggage — none more so than Lord Ronald Sutherland-Leverson-Gower (1845–1916). He first visited the Whitakers in 1889, the same year in which he was involved in the Cleveland Street Scandal, a *cause célèbre* that hit the headlines in 1890. Cleveland Street in London's Fitzrovia had been home to a homosexual brothel which was raided by the police, following which Gower, together with other notable social figures, was implicated. It was even rumoured that the Prince of Wales' eldest son had frequented the establishment. Gower was a friend of John Addington Symonds, a student of Sicily's Grecian past who enjoyed translating classical homoerotic poetry and had penned *A Problem in Greek Ethics*, published privately in 1883 and one of the first books to use the term 'homosexual'. One hundred years later, the book was re-issued with the more revealing title *Male Love*.

Gower dabbled with writing biography, but his real talent lay in sculpture. His most celebrated works are figures of William Shakespeare and four of his most well-known characters including Hamlet — all of which can be found in Stratford-upon-Avon. Gower's contribution to this branch of the arts is detailed in David Getsy's *Sculpture and the Pursuit of a Modern Ideal in Britain*, in which he quotes Addington Symonds, who went to stay with Gower and made the startling statement that he thought that Ronny, as he was known, 'saturates one's spirit in Urningthum of the rankest most diabolical kind'. 'Urningthum' was the word of the day for male homosexuality, whose practitioners were known as Uranians. After his spell in prison for gross indecency, the Victorian era's most famous persecuted Uranian, Oscar Wilde (1854–1900), wrote to his friend Robert Ross that '[to] have altered my life would have been to have admitted that Uranian love is ignoble. I hold it to be noble — more noble than other forms.'

Wilde modelled the character of Lord Henry Wotton in his book *The Picture of Dorian Gray* on Gower. Wotton is Dorian's hedonistic mentor who leads the young man along a path of vice-ridden destruction. Dorian locks his infamous portrait in the attic to age on his behalf, and leads a vain, shallow existence based on a French novel lent to him by Lord Henry. There are certain parallels between the real-life fortunes of Wilde and Gower. On 2 April 1900 Wilde arrived in Palermo; his health had been weakened by hard labour in prison and he was spiralling down towards his demise in November of the same year. Gower and his lover, Frank Hird, had spent the previous five weeks with the Whitakers and missed Wilde's arrival by a few hours.

Raleigh Trevelyan quotes a letter from Tina which states how the garrulous Gower and the effete Hird had just missed the 'embarrassing arrival' of the writer. There is a degree of hypocrisy in this statement given that Tina must have been aware of Gower's sexual preferences, especially as she mentions in the same letter his amusement when teasing Hamilton Aïdé about his supposed naked bath-time antics with a bar of soap, whilst being watched by his German servant. Needless to say, Wilde was not invited to stay at the Villa Malfitano and therefore repaired to The Palms. It is uncertain as to how he managed to pay the bill as he was subsisting on very little income while he badgered his publisher for payment. Wilde was living above his means, as attested by his final days in Paris in the grimy Hôtel d'Alsace, the *pension* he was forced to live in when the money ran out.

In another letter to Robert Ross, Wilde describes the eight days he spent in Palermo using the pronoun 'we', suggesting that he had assistance in coping with the financial expenditure. It is clear from the letter, dated 16 April 1900 and sent from Rome, that he had very much enjoyed his stay, finding beauty in the orange and lemon groves of the Conca d'Oro and the mosaics in the Palatine Chapel. Oscar also provides his friend with a description of the tomb of Frederick II, the Holy Roman Emperor, which lies in the city's cathedral: ' … I really knelt before the huge porphyry sarcophagus in which Frederick II lies. It is a sublime bare monstrous thing, blood-coloured, and held up by lions, who have caught some of the rage of the great Emperor's restless soul.'

Wilde was shown around the building by a young seminarian called Giuseppe Loverde who, when quizzed by the author, explained that he had joined the church due to his family's poverty, a reason that Wilde thought 'singularly mediaeval [sic]'. Wilde became somewhat infatuated with Giuseppe as his letter reveals:

> I told him to be comforted, because God used poverty often as a means of bringing people to Him, and used riches never, or but rarely. So Giuseppe was comforted, and I gave him a little book of devotion, very pretty and with far more pictures than prayers in it; so of great service to Giuseppe, whose eyes are beautiful. I also gave him many *lire*, and prophesied for him a Cardinal's hat, if he remained very good and never forgot me. He said he never would: and indeed I don't think he will, for every day I kissed him behind the high altar.

Palermo provided a short respite from the embarrassment he felt in France when frequently bumping into old acquaintances who remembered him at the height of his fame and powers. Secretly, Wilde may have been grateful that he had missed meeting Gower at the Villa Malfitano where Gower was a treasured house guest and Wilde nothing but an ex-criminal interloper. The Palms was an anonymous bolt-hole and Ragusa was shrewd and polite enough to extend to Wilde the same hospitality he would show any guest. Doubtless, Wilde would have brought his flamboyant yet faded glamour to the hotel. As more guests from the European *beau monde* walked through Ragusa's always open doors, the proprietor was beginning to realise that his establishment had to keep pace with changing fashions in order to remain at the forefront of Palermitan life. Looking around the property, he decided that it was time for Benjamin Ingham's tired structure and décor to undergo a revamp that would reflect the tastes of the Belle Époque.

3

THE WILDER REACHES OF THE BELLE ÉPOQUE

As Europe revelled in a time of peace, so the arts were allowed to flourish. Certain styles that had taken root in the continent's consciousness now began to proliferate in all aspects of fashionable society. Art Nouveau and its cousins, *Jugendstil* and Modernism, became the normalised reaction to stilted academic concepts. Not content to influence only architectural methods, Art Nouveau embraced everything from jewellery to graphic and furniture design. A building could now represent a total work of art, with the edifice and its contents reflecting the prevalent school of thought. In Italy, the Modernist movement was rechristened *stile Liberty* in homage to the style of Archibald Knox whose designs were sold by London's Liberty & Co department store.

By this time, Ernesto Basile (1857–1932) was already an architect of note. In 1891 he had taken over the completion of Palermo's Teatro Massimo from his father, Giovanni Battista. The imposing theatre is the largest edifice of this type in Italy and was constructed in the neo-classical style, true to Giovanni's vision for the building. His son's public association with *stile Liberty* ostensibly began with a submission for the reconstruction of the Palazzo Montecitorio, the seat of the Italian Chamber of Deputies in Rome. Emerging from his residence at The Palms, Francesco Crispi organised a competition for the Chamber's reconstruction and Basile won the right to pursue his ideas. Given Crispi had spent much time in Palermo, it takes only a small leap of the imagination to conclude that the then Interior Minister and future Prime Minister would have met Basile within the confines of the hotel, giving them the opportunity to share opinions on politics and architecture.

Frustratingly, the constraining ties of Byzantine red tape halted progress and the project did not receive the official go-ahead until 1903. It was clear from the outset that Basile intended on fusing the extant classical and Baroque elements with much Art Nouveau imagery, especially noticeable in the debating chamber itself. Terry Kirk, in his work *The Architecture of Modern Italy*, has described the Montecitorio's redevelopment as one of the most important moments of early modernism in architecture. Considering the complexities of transforming the country's seat of power, it was a much less daunting task to adapt The Palms in a similar manner.

The most obvious alteration to the exterior, as it existed prior to 1907, was the removal of the *jardin d'hiver* abutting the western end of the hotel. The substantial glasshouse extension and enclosed area harbouring exotic plant species were sacrificed to the overarching Liberty scheme. The hotel entrance was reimagined in the iconic manner it retains today. The pillars surrounding the doorway now supported the curved opaque awning with its gently flared skirt, protecting new arrivals from the excesses of the island's climate as the porters unloaded their baggage.

The principal impact of the alterations, however, was felt inside the building, with three specific areas being of particular note. The ceiling of the Sala Caminetto, which the hotel has recently been using as an events and conference room, was inlaid with an intarsia technique of wooden segments. Despite Sicily's own traditions in this field of decorative art, Basile employed English craftsmen to interlace the cross-sections between patterned end panels. His use of wood had already been evident in Rome's Chamber of Deputies, where elegant arched niches sweep upwards towards intarsia strips supporting the pictorial frieze entitled *The Italian People*.

The foyer of The Palms was equally impressively remastered. The plaster ceiling was heavily inset and the floor laid with seamless marble. The faux columns on the walls were designed to support delicately branching brass wall lights; the arch separating the marble staircases leading up to the salons was also used to frame a large mirror with a rail-pattern design divided by thin brass bars. The overall effect of this decoration has been maintained throughout the ensuing decades. A bust of Wagner has long sat in the archway vetting the guests and proclaiming his connection to the establishment.

The Sala Specchi, as the Italian name suggests, is lined with mirrored decoration, ranging from unadorned reflective panels to ornately embossed strips of glass, with forms taken from nature and geometry, reminiscent of the work of Scottish architect and designer Rennie Mackintosh, but more elaborate in design. The luxuriant radiance in the room is enhanced by a transparent ceiling in a grid format, set back from the curved panels above the architraving, all of which is bordered in gold and white.

The substantial makeover was designed to enhance the hotel's reputation, which was already riding high in aristocratic and intellectual circles. Dignitaries and wealthy merchants mingled amongst the statues, sofas and pillars of the entrance lobby. It was easy to bump into someone you wished to meet, or indeed avoid, as The Palms had become the social destination of most significance in central Palermo. Affairs of business or the heart were frequently settled within its confines, even if the symbolic gesture of a slap with a glove was enough to quash the ambitions of a rival.

One such notable frequenter of the hotel was Ignazio Florio Jr. (1869–1957), the inheritor of a vast fortune in shipping, banking, viticulture, tuna fishing and salt extraction. In fact, if Sicily had an important resource, Florio usually had an interest in mining, catching, processing or shipping it. He was a cultured man who had travelled widely and was familiar with several European languages. Florio had even been tempted to dabble as a *hotelier*, also employing Basile to convert Palermo's Villa Igiea from a proposed tuberculosis sanatorium to a hotel. Amongst those more concerned with the arts, he is best remembered for his activities as an impresario at the Teatro Massimo and for his foundation of the free-speaking newspaper, *L'Ora*.

The Florio name is most associated today with Marsala wine, as it adorns the eponymously titled bottles produced by the winery Florio, founded in 1833. We have seen however that it was once associated with a vast array of entrepreneurial activities. By the end of the first decade of the twentieth century, Florio was at the height of his considerable powers, but rivals were common and the family could no longer command the market in the same manner as the dynasty's founding father, Vincenzo. Regular meetings and social gatherings at The Palms were but one demonstration of how Florio enjoyed the wealth of his family fortune but, without adopting prudence, he ran the risk of it draining away.

Such occasions were seen as a way to make connections and promote further enterprise, although they did not always have the desired effect. Nevertheless, Florio knew he had a privileged position and made contributions to aid earthquake relief in Messina after the catastrophic tremors of 1908, whilst also endowing a home for the blind in Palermo with his considerable largesse. These altruistic efforts were tempered with extravagances that included the latest tailored clothing imported from Meyer & Mortimer of London and frequent trips on his yacht, the *Ettore Fieramosca*.

Florio took his business too seriously and was too involved in the minutiae of cutting-edge development to be called a playboy, but his greatest weakness was the opposite sex. As Belle Époque Palermo indulged the last excesses of its aristocratic class, and elaborate carriages or the newest automobiles disgorged the glitterati of Europe at the steps of the Teatro Massimo, Florio took every opportunity to pursue his womanising habits. He had married Franca Jacona (1873–1950) in 1893, but that did not curb his wandering eye.

Franca, a beauty of Mediterranean complexion, with green eyes and lustrous black hair, was the daughter of Baron Pietro Jacona della Motta and Costanza Notarbartolo di Villarosa from the renowned Palermitan family. Her fellow socialites called her the 'Queen of Palermo' and she did not lack admirers, including Kaiser Wilhelm II, the poet Gabriele D'Annunzio and the portrait painter Giovanni Boldini. Although she resisted temptation, Florio, on the other hand, paid heavily for his infidelities. Expensive diamond trinkets and bejewelled rings would be proffered in an attempt to smooth over his most recent indiscretion. They were frequently thrown back in his face or dashed to the ground by an irate Franca who, once calm, would retrieve them and realise she had little choice but to accept them and carry on as before, in the hope that the same scene would not be repeated.

When not placating an angry wife, Florio was fending off his amatory rivals. On one memorable occasion in 1912 he confronted Count

Arrivabene in the hall of The Palms. A simple slap with a glove was not sufficient on this occasion and a full-blown duel took place with that most ancient of weapons, the sword, albeit in this case a fencing foil. The cause of the conflict was Vera Papadopoli Aldobrandini (1883–1946), the daughter of a wealthy Venetian banker, who had married Gilberto Arrivabene. A portrait by Umberto Brunelleschi from 1920 shows her in all her Art Nouveau glory, modelling a flower-patterned coat and saucer hat, her waist cinched by a black belt held by a large oval buckle, all against a stylised mountain landscape.

The bloodless duel and the resulting scandal caused Arrivabene and Vera to separate. It seems that having her two admirers fight in medieval combat for her long-lost honour was not dramatic enough to dissuade Vera from continuing her liaison with Florio. Ultimately, though, the emotional upheaval took its toll and Vera was seemingly plagued by opiate addiction for the latter part of her life. The road for the Florios would also be strewn with potholes; despite Ignazio's best efforts his businesses appeared to be cursed with the worst kind of luck.

One enterprise after another hit the rocks. Explanations abound, from political choices, to the intervention of northern Italian business interests, the rise of Fascism and even the interference of the Banca Commerciale who took compensatory measures when Florio unsuccessfully sunk much of his capital into renovating Palermo's crumbling docks. His intention had been to re-establish the shipping industry and divert its development from an expanding Genoa, but the attempt simply backfired. Seeking other outlets, Florio invested in banana plantations on the Canary Islands during the 1920s and returned to the family's old associations with tuna fishing — neither venture was successful and the remainder of the firm's capital slowly eroded to nothing.

The 1930s saw the Florios' forced relocation from their apartment in Rome's Via Piemonte to a small hotel in the Porta Pinciana district, where they lost all their servants and were reduced to selling the rest of their jewellery and furniture at auction. A disillusioned and depressed Franca decided to stay with friends in Florence, leaving Ignazio to pine for a wife he used to treat with querulous condescension. Following her death, the one-time raffish dandy returned to Palermo to die a broken man. Gone were the days of high living and *liaisons dangereuses*. Although long overdue, the duelling scandals of the Belle Époque came under legislative scrutiny from 1915 onwards. This was not before time, considering the ludicrous behaviour of Count Ernesto de la Conette and the Marquis Emanuele De Seta who challenged each other no less than seven times in the salons of The Palms.

The newly decorated hotel was not only a beacon for strutting aristocratic peacocks; it also attracted more serious-minded intellectuals. In 1917, the Uruguayan essayist José Enrique Rodó (1871–1917) reserved a room as part of a European tour as correspondent for the Argentinian magazine *Caras y caretas*. Rodó was born in neighbouring Uruguay across the River Plate to a Catalan father whom he had lost at a young age. It was due to this untimely death that Rodó left formal education at the age of fourteen in a bid to support the family. Through a series of relatively humble jobs he continued however to broaden his mind and educate himself for a future he envisioned beyond the mere existence of the daily grind.

Rodó's talent for writing would have been recognised by his superiors in the scribe's office where circumstances forced him to work. By 1895, despite his unassuming start in life, he was integral to the founding of the *Revista Nacional de Literatura y Ciencias Sociales*, a national periodical focusing on literature and social science. This publication brought modernism to Uruguay, mirroring developments in the fields of art and architecture, and brought fame to Rodó with one essay in particular: *Ariel* (1900).

Such was the impact of this lengthy essay that the thinking behind it entered the Spanish language as *Arielismo* and Rodó became the figurehead of Latin cultural values on the continent of America. Rodó used Shakespearian characters to express his ideological concerns, with the text being narrated by the character of Prospero from *The Tempest*. The eponymous sprite represents the guardian of Latin American identity in the face of Caliban's utilitarianism. Caliban is the sharp-tongued incarnation of North American values in direct opposition to Ariel. Rodó was vociferous in his condemnation of the pragmatic philosophy that placed utility above all else in the search for human happiness.

Rodó believed the concept of utilitarianism forced individuals into a degree of specialisation that ignored the holistic and therefore stunted their educational growth. A human being could not be complete without an understanding of life through broader knowledge, thus avoiding the mediocrity he saw in a way of thinking that led to genius in one field and incompetence in another. These ideas even led to an attack on the state of democracy as he saw it: 'Hanging over democracy is the weighty accusation of guiding humanity, mediocritising it, towards the Sacred Empire of utilitarianism.' These are powerful words, not necessarily intended as an attack on democratic values, but rather a plea to avoid the dumbing down of the masses in the hope that those most capable in society could raise the holistic educational standards of the populace.

Rodó warned of *nordomanía*, South America's obsessional concentration on all things North American, particularly developments in the US. The Spanish-American War of 1898 and the resentment he felt at the US's interference in Cuba led to the publication of *Ariel*. The Cuban crisis was also a low point in Hispanic self-esteem which he did much to raise. It is no surprise that Rodó turned to politics, and from 1902 served in the National Chamber of Representatives until he clashed with José Battle, the then President of Uruguay, who was at the forefront of a measure to remove religious emblems from medical institutions. Rodó was so incensed by the measure that in 1906 he penned *Liberalismo y Jacobinismo*, characterising the political manoeuvre as 'Jacobonism'. The fallout in Uruguayan society was considerable and his enemies grew.

Consistently concerned with the deep connections between Latin America, Spain and the rest of Latin Europe, Rodó was long overdue a trip to the continent — a job as correspondent for the Argentinian magazine gave him the perfect excuse. His words from Naples illustrate the link he felt with Italy and especially the south's profound association with Spain: 'In Spain. And this first impression is corroborated as the soul of the city gives us a glimpse of its secrets and the evocation of the secular stones awakes in our imagination the heroic Spain that passed through here and let its spirit bloom.' From Naples, he travelled down to Palermo, warmed by the April sun, and deposited his bags in The Palms.

Rodó's health had never been robust, and he also suffered from depression, but his European trip had been a tonic, that is, until the night of 30 April 1917. The writer was rushed to the San Saverio hospital with a severe abdominal pain. The medics were unable to alleviate the terrible stabbing agony he felt in his stomach and he died at ten o'clock the following morning. A medical report on his death attributed his demise to typhus and nephritis. The latter can be ascribed to either an autoimmune disorder or infections and toxins that affect the major organs in the body.

This seems a perfectly plausible explanation for his death, but a few conspiracy theorists have hinted at foul play through poisoning, and any detective worth his salt would have found ample motive for a would-be assassin by reading through Rodó's essays. The medical report is still kept in Palermo's municipal archive but its pages lack detail and, by modern standards, it is rather incomplete, even omitting the cemetery of his burial. In fact, the body of the forty-five-year-old Rodó was embalmed and subsequently interred in the graveyard at Rotoli until 1920 when his remains were repatriated to Uruguay. The lasting trace of Rodó's presence at the hotel is a plaque from the government and people of Uruguay fixed to the side of the building which borders Via Mariano Stabile. It attests to the fact that this is where Rodó stayed and wrote his last pages, calling him 'el insigne escritor' (the distinguished writer).

Two years after Rodó's body was safely back in Uruguay, Benito Mussolini (1883–1945) came to power in Italy after thirty thousand of his supporters marched on Rome and demanded the resignation of the Liberal Prime Minister, Luigi Facta. The king, Victor Emmanuel III, denied Facta's request for martial law and controversially appointed Mussolini in his place, opening the gates to a Fascist dictatorship. *Il Duce* was soon provoking international incidents, notably the 1923 invasion of Corfu by Italian forces. As John Julius Norwich has pointed out in his book *Sicily: A Short History from the Ancient Greeks to Cosa Nostra*, 'the rise of Benito Mussolini left Sicily unimpressed. The island had always been considered the least Fascist part of Italy; in the elections of 1921 the party won no seats there at all.'

It was only after Mussolini's power-grab that the island eventually succumbed to elected Fascists, although the killing of Socialist parliamentarian Giacomo Matteotti severely dented their reputation. Matteotti had denounced the methods by which votes were garnered and suffered a grisly end at the hand of his kidnappers who stabbed him several times with a carpenter's file. His body was found in Riano, outside Rome. The resulting furore could have seen the end of the Fascists but the opposing forces were not quick enough to seize their opportunity.

Watching the rise of Mussolini and his army of Blackshirts from a small villa in the hills of Cefalù was a notorious Englishman, Aleister Crowley (1875–1947). Crowley had moved to Sicily in 1920 in a bid to establish his self-styled 'Abbey of Thelema'. No stranger to controversy, Crowley had decamped to the US during World War I where he became involved in the pro-German movement. It has been revealed in subsequent biographies that he had supposedly used this guise of a turncoat Englishman to infiltrate German intelligence. Questions of national allegiance, though, were the least of Crowley's alleged wrongdoings, which ranged from drug dependency, bisexuality and Satanism to soliciting, sadomasochism and the blood sacrifice of animals.

Amid all the hysteria, there was some truth to these claims. The son of deeply religious Plymouth Brethren parents, Crowley was nonetheless the product of an establishment upbringing, having briefly boarded at the prestigious Tonbridge School so hated by E.M. Forster. Between 1895 and 1898 he studied philosophy at Cambridge where he contracted syphilis from his enthusiastic use of prostitutes and experimented with same-sex partners, notably Herbert Charles Pollitt. Pollitt was President of the Cambridge Footlights, and would go on to become a female impersonator known as Diane de Rougy. The pair shared an interest in the type of art and literature that bourgeois society considered decadent.

At a time when exotic locations were difficult and expensive to reach, Crowley was incredibly well-travelled. His first mystical moments were experienced in Stockholm; he dabbled with the Russian language in St Petersburg and pursued alchemy in Zermatt with an English chemist. Also on his itinerary were the more colourful locations of Mexico and India. In 1900 he settled in Mexico City with a mistress he had selected from the local population; he later claimed it was the Mexicans who had initiated him in the rites of Freemasonry. Via Japan and Hong Kong, he ended up in India which provided a spiritual larder for his esoteric belief systems. Yoga and meditation became part of his everyday routine. Despite the malaria he contracted and various bouts of dysentery, Crowley indulged his more physically active side by attempting to climb K2 — the result was snow-blindness. After all this, a sojourn in Paris followed which must have seemed positively tame, although the man his own mother described as 'the Beast' was capable of turning any location into a wild maelstrom of counter-cultural deeds.

In this sense, Bohemian Paris was the ideal location and it is where he became attached to his future brother-in-law, the painter Gerald Kelly. The pair became acquainted with the sculptor Auguste Rodin, who inspired Crowley to write poems he later published as *Rodin in Rime*. In 1903, Crowley married Rose Kelly, Gerald's sister, and during their honeymoon the couple travelled to Cairo — the destination that inspired Crowley to write *The Book of the Law*, an overblown text which claimed a new age for humanity with the author as its prophet. This pseudo-philosophical treatise full of ritual and mythical characterisation would become the cornerstone of Thelema, his religion. Rose and Aleister asserted that the text was dictated to them by Aiwass, a messenger of Horus.

The relationship with Rose only lasted six years; after having two children, one of whom died in infancy, the couple divorced in 1909. Perhaps unsurprisingly, Rose was suffering from excessive bouts of drinking and, two years later, her former husband had her committed to an institution due to her alcohol-related dementia. Crowley moved on, as he always did, and found other 'scarlet women' to share his rituals, which often included a practice he called 'sex magick'.

Crowley's name is frequently associated with three organisations that represent a *fin de siècle* obsession with esoteric meaning in a rapidly changing world. The first of these was the Hermetic Order of the Golden Dawn, which sought to explore the domains of metaphysics and the occult. Initiates could rise through the order as their experience allowed them to evolve in various practices (ranging from geomancy to scrying and astral travel). Crowley was introduced to the Order by a founder member, Samuel Liddell MacGregor Mathers, who progressed him through the various hierarchies. More sober members of the organisation, including the poet W.B. Yeats, were against his rapid ascent to the upper echelons. Crowley's libertine lifestyle was an issue for many as it seems the pursuit of the esoteric was a serious business and not for the faint-hearted.

While under Mathers' instruction, Crowley attempted something of a coup when he and his mistress tried to seize the organisation's meeting chamber used by the senior 'adepts'. After a court case, the takeover failed. Some biographers have even suggested that the whole scenario was an Intelligence Service plot to undermine Mathers and his power in the Order. Whatever the truth of the matter, Mathers and Crowley went their separate ways and apparently used magic rituals against each other's interests.

Our self-styled magus was subsequently prompted to set up his own group in 1907, labelled with the cryptic title A.˙. A.˙., whose rituals included the downing of peyote, the psychotropic cactus used by the Huichol people in Mexico. Constantly hungering after new experience and a furthering of his knowledge, Crowley then became attracted to the occult order Ordo Templi Orientis. After yet another spat about the rights to shared mystical understanding, he eventually befriended one of the founders, Theodor Reuss. Crowley was nothing if not international in his search for the wisdom of ages, travelling to Berlin in 1912 to be inducted under the name Baphomet by Reuss himself.

All this travelling, drug-taking, sexual experimentation and pursuit of arcane experience was an expensive career choice. From 1914 onwards Crowley was living a precarious financial existence; his flow of inherited money had run dry and he was gratefully accepting donations from followers, whilst using membership fees to keep his head above water. In the US during World War I, his backing for Germany took a journalistic form and he wrote articles for *The Fatherland*, a puppet publication aimed at supporting Kaiser Wilhelm II's government. Researchers who have written on intelligence and the occult, such as Richard Spence, assert that Crowley was a double-agent and the printed pieces were deliberately overwrought.

Back in London, he was labelled a traitor. To add to his woes, his financial difficulties multiplied and his health was affected by a severe bout of asthma. A doctor, presumably unacquainted with his enthusiastic use of narcotics, prescribed him heroin. It would prove his last signpost on the long road to ruin, a route Crowley had been travelling for quite some time. In 1920 he moved back to Paris and through consultation of the *I Ching*, the classic Chinese divination text, decided that Sicily was the answer to his problems, although finding somewhere cheap to live was probably more of a consideration.

Crowley's prolific writing output, which always sought to advance his dubious theories, ultimately culminated in what were called *The Holy Books of Thelema*, at the heart of which was his Egyptian *Book of the Law*. Cefalù, on the northern coast of the island, was his chosen destination for the Abbey of Thelema, a grandiose title for a very simple villa. His American mistress, Leah Hirsig, accompanied him with their new baby daughter, and they were soon joined by another paramour, Ninette Shumway. The warring women would occasionally prove intolerable to Crowley, who used their disagreements as an excuse for fleeing to Palermo.

Cefalù, now a popular holiday resort, was once a simple fishing village with few amenities; anything beyond the bare necessities would have required a trip to the island's capital. The essentials may have been the freshest available, but Crowley was a man used to the finer things in life and they were only to be had in Palermo. Despite budgetary constraints, he refused to stay in a simple *pension* and used to head for The Palms. For 'the Beast', the city was not only a gastronomic destination and a transport hub, but also a sexual supermarket.

Crowley would roam the streets of Palermo in search of prostitutes of both sexes that he could pay to take part in his sex magick; he would not have been short of choice. The island's juxtaposition of rich and poor, so evident when the British merchants built their extravagant villas, had barely improved since the start of the 1920s. In fact, Italy was undergoing a wave of unprecedented mass migration to the US, and of the 4.5 million who emigrated between 1880 and 1930, over a quarter were from Sicily. These figures do not even take into consideration the large numbers who moved to Argentina and Brazil. A cursory glance at the Buenos Aires phonebook or the names on the shirts of the national football team is enough to indicate the Italian presence. Those forced by their situation into a new life overseas were often from the villages of the interior, but not exclusively. Some, by choice or circumstance, failed to make it to the Americas and were, instead, drawn to the big conurbations of Catania and Palermo.

The capital was taking in a jobless itinerant population of rural poor who were being crammed into districts already suffering from deprivation, particularly in the Albergheria. To make matters worse, World War I had not been kind to Sicily. The island had suffered from blocked export markets, and the consequent downturn in economic activity had affected those reliant on the kind of casual income gained from day labouring. It also encouraged the black market to flourish, creating a set of conditions designed to facilitate the spread of an already burgeoning mafia. Although the country emerged intact from the ruins of war, it did so at a cost, especially in the south.

Italian prime minister Vittorio Emmanuele Orlando, a former denizen of The Palms, represented Italy at the post-conflict Paris Peace Conference in 1919. Orlando had long been associated with the mafia, a fact he felt no compunction to hide. In one memorable speech in 1925 he gave a defence of values he championed as 'Sicilian', finishing with the declaration that he was honoured to be thought of as a *mafioso*: 'If by the word "Mafia" we understand a sense of honour pitched in the highest key; a refusal to tolerate anyone's prominence or overbearing behaviour ... if such feelings and such behaviour are what people mean by "the Mafia"... I declare that I am a *mafioso*, and proud to be one.' People turned to the mafia, as they still do, in order to obtain some form of employment; however, in the years following the war, it was a question of driving hunger that forced many into the arms of organised crime and others to turn to the oldest profession. The *Cosa Nostra* loves a void that it can fill, offering a dubious promise of better times and companionship.

Crowley's reckless world had met the underbelly of Sicilian society, a world obscured by varying degrees of shade, both metaphorical and literal. The urban chancers of the Albergheria inhabited streets so narrow that a corpulent visitor could touch houses on either side of the rutted paving. It is easier to imagine a curiously attired Crowley picking up a whey-faced youth and sneaking his would-be partner into the hotel, than it is to picture him ritualising his sexual activity in the crumbling surroundings of a pseudo-squat in the district once home to the eighteenth-century charlatan Cagliostro. Although, if he was aware of the supposed Count Cagliostro's origins in this area, Crowley may well have been attracted by the man's self-promoting stories of alchemy, psychic healing and seduction.

The rise of the Fascists would prove problematic for Crowley, who was clearly the type of man they considered degenerate. Activities in Cefalù had heightened as followers were attracted to his 'Abbey'. It is not unreasonable to think that denunciations may have led to the monitoring of his activities, especially at The Palms, where he was no longer part of a close-knit grouping that seldom ventured beyond their own milieu. As the Thelemite community grew, his rituals became more involved and outlandish. The walls of the villa (his Abbey) were adorned with pictures of goats and semi-naked women cavorting in orgiastic fervour, an enticement to celebrants. Crowley signed his frescoes with a letter 'A' and a pair of rounded legs, designed to represent a penis. In the centre of the main room, which he had turned into a temple, he placed a table that he called 'The Throne of the Great Beast'.

Processions, in full regalia, around his rented property marked out bizarre paths of esoteric significance and, when observed from afar, were enough to alarm the neighbours. As Giuseppe Quatriglio has pointed out in his book *L'isola dei miti* (*The Island of Myths*), the locals were both repelled and attracted by the secretive figure of Crowley. Their impressions were confirmed when his party descended from the hills of Santa Barbara for a spot of skinny-dipping. Worse still, in the confines of the villa, dogs and cats were sacrificed and the attendees at his ceremonies were supposedly required to drink the dead animals' blood. It seems that nobody was clearing up after the previous night's debauchery and conditions became unhealthy. The daughter of Ninette Shumway, Poupée, unfortunately died in 1920, but the grieving mother was soon to give birth to another daughter that she christened with the astounding name of Astarte Lulu Panthea.

Notable visitors drawn to Cefalù included American silent-film actress Jane Wolfe who, taking the name 'Soror Estai', became one of Crowley's initiates, not to mention his secretary. She later published her magical experiences as *The Cefalu Diaries*. Others were less enamoured of the rituals, especially the occultist Cecil Frederick Russell, who balked at the same-sex performances he was asked to indulge in, especially as they involved several onlookers.

During the winter of 1921, the Abbey received a visit from another American who, in contrast to Jane Wolfe, was appalled by the scenes she witnessed. Hélène Fraux was Ninette's sister and her job as a nanny brought her into contact with the higher echelons of Detroit society. Any sexual misdemeanours and drug use would not have been on display, keeping her respectable world untainted by vice. Crowley's villa, however, was another matter with its unselfconscious displays of pansexuality and experimentation amid the squalor. Fraux found the situation so sordid that she was moved to report events to the police department in Palermo. It seems this contact finally provoked action and the forces of law and order raided the building, but found nothing they could use to bring charges.

It is also a matter of record that a complaint was made to the British Consul in Palermo, although it seems this report was not acted upon. The Consul at the time was Reginald Gambier MacBean, acting Grand Master of the Ancient and Primitive Rite of Memphis-Misraim for Italy, another esoteric sect. Tobias Churton, in his biography of Crowley, has noted that the two men were initially on amicable terms; it is, therefore, unsurprising that sanctions were not imposed. MacBean would have been useful as a conduit to other diplomatic figures, and Churton specifically cites Walter Alexander Smart who Crowley already knew from his days in New York. Smart would become the inspiration for the Consul in Naples who features in Crowley's 1922 semi-fictionalised work *The Diary of a Drug Fiend*.

The book focuses on Crowley's time at Cefalù and the central characters are based on two more adherents, Mary Butts and Cecil Maitland, although the reality of their stay was far more disturbing than the portrayal in the book. The final nail in the Thelemite coffin was the death of Raoul Loveday, a devotee who brought his wife, Betty May, to

Map of Palermo, 1907, from Bibliographisches Institut AG, Leipzig

The Porta Felice, Palermo

The Ingham bandstand in Piazza Castelnuovo, Palermo

The Anglican Church
opposite The Grand Hôtel
et des Palmes, Palermo

Statue of Joseph (Giuseppe)
Whitaker Jr, known as 'Pip',
in Mozia near Marsala

The Giardino Inglese
with Ernesto Basile's
pavilion, Palermo

The bust of Wagner
in the foyer of The
Grand Hôtel et des
Palmes, Palermo

Franca Florio, Countess
of San Giuliano and
wife of Ignazio Florio
Jr, painted in 1912

The entrance to The
Grand Hôtel et des
Palmes, Palermo

The foyer of
The Grand
Hôtel et
des Palmes,
Palermo

The hall adjoining
the Sala Specchi
in The Grand
Hôtel et des
Palmes, Palermo

The Sala Caminetto with the Ingham fireplace, The Grand Hôtel et des Palmes, Palermo

The mirror disguising the hidden passage in the Blue Room, used until World War II, The Grand Hôtel et des Palmes, Palermo

The Teatro Massimo, Palermo

Mural of judges Falcone and Borsellino
near La Cala, Palermo

Photograph of Raymond Roussel on
display in The Grand Hôtel et des Palmes,
Palermo

Cefalù. Loveday drank from a stream and developed a liver condition that was to kill him, after which Betty felt compelled to tell all to the British press.

Enough was enough. On 23 April 1923, a police officer invited Crowley to accompany him to the Office for Public Security in Palermo. The Beast complied in an uncharacteristically subdued fashion, only to find on arrival that he had been issued an expulsion order from the Interior Ministry itself, signed by the Fascist Minister in charge of the department. Communication of the strange events unfolding must have been rapidly exchanged between a fearful local constabulary and the regional headquarters. As soon as the city's forces of law and order received news of the latest sensation, whether or not they had Crowley under surveillance, they were compelled to report directly to Rome. Mussolini's government stamped the forms and Crowley's life in Sicily was history; his legacy as a *magus* forever to be judged as a disturber of public order in a footnote found in the Fascist archives.

Mussolini had a deep distrust of secret societies and rituals originating from the Masonic world. In his eyes, these were cells that could harbour anti-Fascist thinking and threaten his power. The regime was also aware of Crowley's connection to the intelligence world, which must surely have been a major factor in his removal. By April 1923 Mussolini had already been active in monitoring foreign journalists who portrayed him in an unfavourable light, deporting some of the worst offenders from Italy. The English occultist was seen as a potential spy and propagandist, a Mason and a reprobate.

Crowley departed Sicily alone, a few months before his former landlord at The Palms, Enrico Ragusa, was to breathe his last. The proprietor of the villa, Baron La Calce, promised he would look after Ninette and the child. It seems that not everyone in Cefalù was happy to see the last of the Beast — some locals signed a letter requesting a delay in his expulsion in order to allow time to establish the reason behind his removal which the authorities had refused to divulge. The letter, quoted by Churton, mentions Crowley's fame as a 'poet, scholar and traveller' but, crucially, expounds on his role in bringing visitors to the town who spent money in its shops and businesses. Those who profited from the Abbey of Thelema were prepared to look beyond its excesses.

MacBean, the Consul, had little option but to acquiesce to his own government's requests for information. Shortly before the Fascists had swung into action, two British agents arrived in Cefalù, prompted by the death of Loveday which had been reported in the British newspapers. They were intent on discovering the nature of the activities taking place. In his attempts to break away from convention, Crowley was trouble for everyone. An air of mystery still surrounds his deportation, as to whether it was principally driven by political expediency or the moral high ground; his file however gives the official statement that his sexual activity was 'obscene and perverted'.

Cultural degenerates were not the only targets for a rampant regime, and Mussolini also turned his attention to the mafia. Cesare Mori, a police officer from Pavia, was appointed as the head of the government's task force charged with undermining mafia power. Mori knew Sicily well, having been previously stationed in Trapani. He did not have the rose-tinted vision of the organisation as the noble, almost philanthropic, society that Vittorio Emmanuele Orlando propagated. The historian Christopher Duggan points out that Mori knew the mafia's violent methods were designed to garner money and power for uncompromising individuals.

Mussolini's anti-mafia hitman and his squad arrested thousands in the years following the Fascists' takeover. Charges of criminal association were brought without proof or distinction and the woolly judicial term employed for such charges required no specific evidence. Mori's approach did not shy away from the kind of violence used by his adversaries, including torture and the hostage-taking of a *mafioso*'s wife and children. The idea was to persuade the poverty-stricken Sicilians, who had previously turned to the organisation, to look instead towards the State. Trials of notorious members of the mafia lasted until 1932, three years after the 'Iron Prefect' had left his job in Palermo. He was happy to declare the organisation dead but, as history tells us, this was far from the truth.

The all-powerful government eliminated dissent wherever it arose, dampening down any sparks of revolt before they could ignite and spread. Police investigations served the State and not the populace, as would become evident with the case of the Frenchman Raymond

Roussel (1877–1933). The rather effete writer and poet was an unlikely figure to choose Fascist-era Palermo as a bolthole. He checked into room 224 of The Palms at the beginning of June 1933, accompanied by Charlotte Dufrène, otherwise known as Charlotte Fredez, who took the adjoining room of 226. On the morning of 14 July, Roussel was found dead in his room, in a supine position, on a mattress he had dragged from the bed.

Roussel was born into an affluent Parisian family, whose wealth he inherited at the age of sixteen on the death of his father. This allowed him to pursue his literary and musical ambitions. He is best known for his works *Locus Solus* and *Impressions d'Afrique* (*Impressions of Africa*), both of which have a rigid structure based on the use of homonymic puns. Roussel explained how the use of two similar-sounding words would trigger other homonyms that took the text in diverging directions. He also used a system of brackets that was based on Morse code to encrypt hidden messages within the text. The American poet John Ashbery, who died in 2017, gave a startling description of *Locus Solus* in an introduction he wrote for Foucault's *Death and the Labyrinth*. This snippet gives a flavour of Roussel's experimental eccentricity:

> After an aerial pile driver which is constructing a mosaic of teeth and a huge glass diamond filled with water in which float a dancing girl, a hairless cat, and the preserved head of Danton, we come to the central and longest passage: a description of eight curious *tableaux vivants* taking place inside an enormous glass cage.

Doubtless some of Roussel's imagery was conjured from his prodigious intake of barbiturates which, after affording him much-needed sleep, provided a resulting euphoria. Raymond had long suffered from a form of neurasthenia which caused fatigue, anxiety and lassitude. The barbiturates were both his crutch and his curse. Before leaving Paris, it seems he had put some of his affairs in order, making a last will and testament, although there was a shock in store for his nephew and heir, Michel Ney, the Duke of Elchingen, which would only become apparent on his death. He was surprised to find that he would inherit nothing since there was barely a penny left. Roussel even apologised for this state of affairs which he considered his greatest failure, leaving Ney convinced that the writer knew he was not long for this world.

Charlotte Dufrène, the woman Roussel had taken with him to The Palms, was not his lover, hence the adjoining rooms. She was, as Sicilian writer Leonardo Sciascia memorably describes her in his book on the Roussel case, a '*demimondaine*', a kept woman from the world of the *demimonde*. Her role, aside from settling accounts and monitoring Roussel's health, was to give an acceptable outward appearance to a society who would not tolerate homosexuality — an unmarried liaison was much less of a scandal. Dufrène used a pseudonym to hide from bourgeois society given that she was a convent-educated girl who wanted to conceal her dubious occupation from her parents. She kept a list of Roussel's drug consumption which reads like a pharmacy stocktake. Sciascia, in his *Atti relative alla morte di Raymond Roussel* (*Documents Relating to the Death of Raymond Roussel*) quotes from the extensive list:

> On the 8th, 20 pills of Somnothyril and a bottle of Neurinase: without eating, but in euphoria throughout the whole day. On the 9th, 11 pills of Phanodorme. The 10th, two bottles of Veronidin at 9pm; a good sleep. The 11th, at the same time, 34 pills of Rutonal; three hours sleep and then a 'tremendous euphoria'...

Given this ill-advised intake, repercussions were inevitable. Approximately a month before his death, when Dufrène had departed for Paris to pick up more of his belongings for an extended stay, Roussel was found senseless in his room. The Palms' director, Leopoldo Serena, called the hotel's medic, Professor Lombardo, who managed to bring the unfortunate Frenchman to his senses. Several days later, when Dufrène had already returned, Roussel was discovered in the bathroom, his left wrist slashed and suffering from considerable loss of blood. Lombardo again attended, stitching the wound and tending to the other self-inflicted lesions on his body, although interestingly he never reported this obvious suicide attempt, possibly to avoid any scandalous associations with the hotel's good name.

Dufrène had been pleading with Roussel to cut down his drug use as it was obviously having a deleterious impact on his mental and physical health. By 13 July his nerves were so frayed that, according to the waiter, Tommaso Orlando di Gaetano, he had to be helped from his chauffeur-driven car to the lift and thence to his room — which raises the question as to how he later summoned the strength required to move his mattress from the bed to the floor. To make matters worse, Palermo that day was in full festive mode, celebrating Santa Rosalia, the city's patron saint who had supposedly saved the populace from the plague. Roussel would have heard the uproar from room 224 which, at that time, backed onto Via Mariano Stabile — the street that now displays Rodó's plaque.

He took Sonéryl, a barbiturate that Sciascia affirms was his preferred tablet, given that it assured him a good night's sleep and considerable subsequent euphoria. However, the effect was fatal. The Sicilian author is convinced that Roussel did not intend suicide on this occasion, merely to absent himself from the world for a little while. Raymond had taken far higher doses previously but escaped the ultimate fate.

There are inconsistencies and omissions from the official report that Sciascia quotes from at length. Officially, the porter, Antonio Kreuz, found the prone body of Roussel in his nightshirt, underpants and black socks. At around ten o'clock in the morning, Kreuz had informed Orlando that Roussel had not surfaced and the pair returned to room 224. Everything was silent, apart from the noise of a running shower in room 226. Recently, Raymond had been locking the connecting door to Dufrène's room but he always left the door to the passageway unlocked so that room service could be placed just inside without disturbing him. Uncertain as to how to proceed, and wary of previous events, the two staff members crept away; eventually, Kreuz plucked up the courage to return and enter the room.

In the police report, Dufrène is said to have entered Roussel's room 'at the same time' as Kreuz, although this mysteriously disappears in further judicial memoranda. She even contradicted herself, by firstly declaring that 'they told me of his death', then correcting herself to say she entered the room with the porter. Sciascia posits the idea that a worried Charlotte had already tiptoed along the empty corridor into the adjoining the room and discovered Roussel dead on his mattress. Rather than report matters herself, she had decided to bury her head in the sand until she realised the hotel staff had discovered the truth.

Events are further clouded by the behaviour of Roussel's chauffeur who was not staying at The Palms but who, nonetheless, would have discovered the situation relatively quickly. Instead of making himself known to the authorities, he disappeared from Palermo in very short order — a fact that Dufrène found unremarkable. Furthermore, Roussel's nephew Michel Ney did not hear of his uncle's death from the authorities but from the mouth of the self-same chauffeur. Sciascia does not see this as an altruistic act, but reads the motive as an opportunity to extort money, especially as Ney was unaware of the presence of Dufrène. It is not inconceivable that Dufrène and the chauffeur were in a relationship, or even that Roussel was the chauffeur's lover.

The Fascist authorities were little concerned with decadent *littérateurs* hell-bent on self-destruction. The physician Doctor Rabboni was asked by the appointed judge to examine the body officially, and summed up his statement with the following metaphorical sweep of his hand: 'I consider the above-mentioned Roussel has died a natural death, probably caused by an intoxication of narcotics and sleeping draughts, found in great quantity in the room, therefore I consider an autopsy fruitless.' Frustratingly, the judge's report does not annotate his own questions. We simply have the letters ADR (*a domanda risponde*) meaning a witness was responding to the judge's question, a subtle way of hiding any judicial oversight from inquisitive eyes. It was standard practice.

Other glaring absences include any reference to the chauffeur, a lack of investigation into Charlotte Dufrène's contradictions and any mention of Orlando's observation that Roussel had ejaculated during the night of his death. Remarkably, the whole legal process was wrapped up by the end of the following day. Many questions remain unanswered, questions that an autopsy would have been useful in solving. However, the path Roussel was treading could only lead to one destination. He had sworn to Dufrène that he would seek help in a Swiss sanatorium but quickly reneged on attempts to cut back on barbiturates. Leonardo Sciascia is one of the champions of the theory that Roussel had not intended to kill himself, whereas Michel Ney was convinced that his actions were deliberate. Perhaps the answer lies somewhere in between and the Frenchman was playing Russian roulette with his own life, knowing full well that sooner or later his body would not be able to withstand the elephantine amounts of narcotics to which it was being subjected.

During the course of our own reading on the topic, we have consulted various texts. In the Spanish version of Sciascia's *Atti relativi*, the translator, Julio Reija, appends his own thoughts on the matter. He makes the convincing case that the suicide of Sciascia's brother may have led the writer to seek the absolution of Raymond Roussel, although Sciascia's ire is chiefly aimed at the lackadaisical investigation by Mussolini's forces of law and order. The death of an effeminate dilettante drug addict mattered little to the men who could sentence hard-bitten *mafiosi* to years in prison.

One man intrigued by the Roussel case was the eccentric Italian writer Baron Agostino Fausto La Lomia (1905–78). In her book *Alla scoperta dei segreti perduti della Sicilia (In Search of Sicily's Lost Secrets)*, Clara Serretta makes the claim that La Lomia's favourite room in The Palms was 224 – as we know, the scene of Roussel's demise. He shared his many stays at the hotel with a pet blackbird he called Don Turiddu Capra and a cat who accompanied him everywhere, going by the equally glorious name of Sua Eccellenza Referendario Paolo Annarino.

La Lomia boasted of his popularity and, as if to prove it, spent time in his room writing letters to himself which he duly took to the reception for delivery. He would subsequently return and collect the post he had penned hours earlier. The Baron was also famous for his amorous conquests, not all of which were gained through his charm and individuality. It seems he would pay beautiful women to spend the night in his hotel room. One anecdote, which appeared in an article for the Italian national newspaper, *La Repubblica*, tells of chambermaid and room service staff finding La Lomia on his knees after such a night. As if completely drained by the experience, he turned to them asking for help.

The aristocrat was born in 1905, and inherited palaces in Canicattì and Palermo. Amongst a long list of his unconventional acts was the establishment in 1922 of the Accademia del Parnaso (the Academy of Parnaso), a genial society located in Canicattì and designed to promote poetry and other cultural pursuits. However, the statutes for entry to the Academy were as bizarre as its subsequent events. The society deemed a 'poet' anyone who had come of age and believed in eternal love along with the faithfulness of women. Another statute recognised the muse in anyone who was not happy with simply having the right answer but, furthermore, needed to try and win a battle. There were other requirements in a similar Quixotesque and quasi-medieval vein.

Members of the Academy were taken from all levels of social standing and included illiterate peasants, a priest, a lawyer and even a local thug. The priest owned a donkey that, with the addition of wings as a poetic gesture, became the symbol of the society. With members convinced that further embellishments were needed, a lion was added to the crest and the design was sent to Palermo for printing on to stationery. The printers only had the impression of a dog to hand so they substituted the king of beasts with man's best friend. Unfazed, La Lomia and his friends issued a decree declaring the dog to be a lion, irrespective of appearances.

Meetings of the Academy would see aphorisms, dialectal poetry, epigraphs and satire exchanged between the associates who glorified in the title of 'Arcadians'. To give a semblance of weight to the proceedings, the Baron liked to claim that the origins of the gathering dated back to the time of Charles V, the Holy Roman Emperor, and that his Spanish grandees were the first to set up this tribute to Parnassus, the sacred mountain of the Muses. Underlying the superficial appearance of such an institution was a subtle satire directed towards the Fascists. The honour of high-level Arcadian was only given to peasant poets and local vagabonds, with the likes of Nobel Laureate Luigi Pirandello receiving a mere honorary membership at the lowest level. Clearly, Pirandello was never moved to become an actual participating member.

Gaetano Savatteri, who has written wonderfully on La Lomia in his book *I siciliani* (*The Sicilians*), feels that this inverted hierarchy was a rebuff to the Fascist desire for fanfare, status and vainglorious decoration. The Academy even landed itself in hot water with the authorities over a debate concerning the Italian ancestry of Christopher Columbus. In Spanish, Columbus' name is Cristóbal Colón and La Lomia used to enjoy the kudos of name-dropping Gian Francesco Collion, one of the supposed originators of his society from the days of

Spanish rule whom he considered a relative of the famous explorer. The Baron and his friends concluded that all Colóns and variants thereof had to be Spanish, an opinion that eventually reached the hallowed grounds of Spain's Salamanca University. This assertion filtered back to Italy and must have annoyed the Genoese, who proudly claim him as their own. As a consequence, the Fascist authorities were sent to investigate the society.

Pouring further oil on already troubled waters was the decision to award higher Arcadian status to Mussolini's regional prefect, who soon worked out that his fellow members at the same level were simple peasants, not to mention homeless wanderers. He refused to brush aside the slight and issued the Academy a list of subjects that members were forbidden to take lightly. If La Lomia found his humour restricted politically, he was less circumspect with matters concerning death. Years later, in 1969, the *Giornale di Sicilia* newspaper carried a formal notice announcing the death and funeral of Sua Eccellenza Referendario Paolo Annarino; the announcement of the cat's death was made by an undoubtedly sorrowful Turridu Capra.

There is no reason to think that La Lomia took his faithful pet's death lightly; it was just his way of showing respect and grief. Absurdist humour was his vehicle and defence mechanism for dealing with life. He is often famously quoted as saying that the silly things in life should be enjoyed in order to make the world one's own. He really thought that everything in this world was frivolous to a lesser or greater degree, although it seems he believed true life existed only in death. His black humour was most visible when he staged his own mock funeral in 1967 which he attended with heart beating and breath in his lungs, still very much full of life. The Baron was pictured next to his tomb, which was only missing the inscription of the inevitable date to come. A suitably extravagant band played the distinctive brass music that can be heard to this day at Sicilian funerals and he supplied all his guests with almond pastries. His excuse for the charade was the fact that one should only think about death when one was happy.

La Lomia's plans for his real funeral were even more lavish. He wanted over four hundred guests, who would be served ice-cream and the traditional Sicilian dessert, *cassata*. Instructions were also left for professional mourners to be drawn from various countries of the Mediterranean. One of them had to represent a notary with a crooked hand, one a Christian Democrat deputy with a pitchfork and another a banker with a noose. These *tableaux vivants* were designed to symbolise the impounding of his palazzo in Palermo, one of the reasons he spent so much time in The Palms.

The article in *La Repubblica* mentioned earlier contradicts somewhat Clara Serretta's assertion that 224 was his favourite room, believing it to be 124 instead. The newspaper purports that the reason for his choice was the fact that he believed he had been conceived in the room. To further cloud the issue, we have also seen the Ambasciatori Hotel given as the site of his conception. Whatever the truth may be, the confusion is redolent of a man who liked to obfuscate and satirise reality, especially when it concerned the momentous events of life and death. He declared himself a fervent Christian, whilst at the same time behaving like a Lothario. A picture exists of La Lomia with a large crucifix around his neck and, as if to counterbalance this perception, a Panama hat with a feather jutting from the band at a jaunty angle. His abundant hair and beard soften the collar of a cape which is draped over his shoulders in a Bohemian manner. Sadly, the Baron's actual funeral did not live up to expectations and barely fifty people attended an event that did not reflect his wishes.

The backdrop to La Lomia's creatively eccentric zenith was the Fascist era, a period that threatened the satirical free-thinking meetings of the Academy. Despite heading up such a bizarre association during dangerous times, the aristocrat escaped any serious repercussions due to his noble standing in society. Not all visitors to The Palms were so fortunate. In 1937, the Italian fleet was on manoeuvres in the Tyrrhenian Sea and using Palermo harbour as its base. Sicily and Sardinia had become strategically important owing to their location in relation to the Iberian Peninsula, and Mussolini's government had unwisely become embroiled in the Spanish Civil War (1936–39).

Francisco Franco (1892–1975), the figurehead of the Spanish Right who led his troops stationed in Morocco across the Straits of Gibraltar to march on Madrid after acclaiming a military rebellion, had lobbied the government in Rome for military assistance. Italian agents on the ground in Spain had already forewarned the Fascists back in Italy that an uprising was imminent. Galeazzo Ciano, Mussolini's playboy son-in-law, supplied the planes that shuttled the soldiers to the mainland, although three were lost through mechanical failure before they even reached Morocco. Prominent Italian Generals, notably Mario Roatta, warned the government that its forces would be drawn into Spain's vortex with dire consequences.

Little by little, despite Mussolini's feigned disinterest in Spanish matters, Italy did increase its involvement through naval and air assistance in addition to the CTV (*Corpo truppo volontario*, the Corps of Volunteer Troops). Evidence from the field also reveals that regular Italian units were deployed as well as the aforementioned Fascist militia. To the south of Sicily, the country had also become embroiled in expansionist colonialism in Libya and Abyssinia. To add fuel to this combustible mix, certain members of the War Ministry, especially Alberto Pariani, the Under-Secretary, were increasingly convinced that conflict with the British and French was on the horizon.

It is no wonder that the Italian fleet had chosen this moment to make a show of strength off the coast of Sicily. It was the year that Mussolini had returned to the island to promote agricultural reform in another attempt at rallying the half-hearted populace to the Fascist banner. No doubt he had an eye on the grain that would be required during a time of war. The navy had recently launched two new battleships, the *Littorio* and *Vittorio Veneto*, the most modern of the Regia Marina (Royal Navy) taskforce. Major treaties of 1922 and 1930 were torn to shreds and there was a rush towards rearmament.

The Spanish Civil War had made the British look in depth at the Italian navy's Mediterranean capability. In the *Mediterranean Historical Review*, Michael Alpert makes the claim that Britain was aware that it had stretched its seaborne competence in defence of far-flung outposts of Empire and therefore had a lack of strength from the Straits of Gibraltar to Cyprus should its forces become engaged in a fight with the Italians. Mussolini's government resented Britain's refusal to recognise its growing naval power and subsequent rights in its own backyard. Consequently, it threw money at anyone who had a shared ideology and was prepared to stand up to British interests in the region, especially anti-British Nationalists in Malta and Egypt. Furthermore, the Regia Marina dominated routes from Sicily to Spain, leaving the Republican forces aligned against Franco at the mercy of a quasi-blockade.

Agents from all the active powers in the region were covertly at work on the ground, gathering intelligence in each other's territories. Information on naval movements in the Tyrrhenian Sea and the capability of new ships would have been vital for those charged with uncovering the nature of the threat presented by a potential enemy. In 1937, an Englishman, whose real identity still remains a mystery, checked into The Palms. By this time, the hotel must have been under constant surveillance by OVRA (Organizzazione per la Vigilanza e la Repressione dell'Antifascismo, the Organisation for Vigilance and Repression of Anti-Facism). Mussolini's secret service had been initially charged with monitoring anti-Fascist activities, but was used during the war and its prelude as an intelligence agency actively engaged in rooting out spies and creating double agents. The mysterious Briton, ensconced in room 322, attracted the wrong sort of attention. He was found in a pool of blood on the bedroom floor with a dagger protruding from his back. The case was conveniently hushed up by the authorities as Europe moved inevitably towards war.

4

FROM WORLD WAR TO MAFIA WARS

It took nine months for Mussolini to declare war; despite Italy's 'Pact of Steel' with Hitler's Germany, *Il Duce* was warned of the consequences that an early entry into the conflict would have for the underprepared nation. Chief in advising caution was Marshal Badoglio, who knew his troops would lack the necessary equipment. By 10 June 1940 however, everything appeared to be pointing towards success for the Axis powers as one nation after another fell to the German advance. Mussolini was tempted by the possibilities of this territorial grab and he threw Italy's weight behind Hitler's forces.

The situation in 1943 was far from the glorious imperial victory envisioned by the Fascists when they had entered the fray three years previously. Initially, Italy had turned its envious eye on the North African coast and it was with the aim of making the likes of Tunisia and Egypt into an Italian fiefdom that Mussolini ordered his troops across the Mediterranean. The campaign went badly wrong and the defeated army was routed by the British. Doubtless to the dictator's annoyance, it was the German Afrika Korps who came to their rescue, although even Rommel's troops were defeated at El Alamein in November 1942.

The focus of attention now turned to Sicily. As Churchill pointed out, it must have been obvious to all that the Allied invasion would come through the island, so a diversionary measure was needed to persuade Hitler and Mussolini otherwise. The covert distraction came in the form of Operation Mincemeat which involved the corpse of a vagrant Welshman dressed as a major in the British army. Ten weeks prior to the invasion of Sicily, 'Major William Martin' was dropped into the waters off the Iberian Peninsula where his floating body was spotted by a local fisherman. The Spanish authorities rifled through the briefcase still attached to the body and found supposedly compromising information.

The Allies were banking on the fact that Franco would pass this documentation to Hitler, despite his theoretical neutrality. True to form, the Spanish authorities did their duty and the Germans took possession of information stating that Sardinia and Southern Greece were to be the invasion points, and that Sicily would only be half-heartedly attacked as a diversionary ploy. In July 1943 Axis troops were deployed to reflect Major Martin's deadly indiscretion — the commanders of the German and Italian soldiers stationed in Sicily were only expecting a cursory skirmish as a prelude to the main event elsewhere.

To add fuel to the combustible mixture of disinformation and expectation, it was clear to Allied intelligence that all was not well between the Germans and their Sicilian hosts. The British Secret Intelligence Service (SIS) Handbook on all matters concerning the island noted that there was no love lost between the locals and the foreign troops stationed there. Germans were blamed for food shortages as Sicilians believed preference was given to export; conversely, Hitler's soldiers looked down upon the islanders whom they considered little more than illiterate brutes. The SIS text even concluded that Italian involvement in the war had encouraged Sicilian separatist leanings. The natural assumption was that a war-weary populace might welcome the forthcoming invasion.

Those working in the field of covert operations were keen to exploit any feelings of resentment and rebellion on the island. The British and Americans played to their strengths, trying to cultivate influence in two separate directions. For the class-obsessed British, it was natural that they should focus on fostering relations with the aristocracy and those wealthy businessmen who once graced the foyer of The Palms. The Americans drew on the more intimate familial connections already in place through mass migration to the US.

On the night of 9 July 1943, 2,500 ships made for the south-east coast of Sicily, a far larger convoy than the expected distraction, for a landing code-named Operation Husky. Amongst the thousands of regular troops were small groupings of intelligence officers who had been fomenting the aforementioned networks. One such was a team of American Naval Intelligence lieutenants whose story is told in Tim Newark's book, *The Mafia at War*. The team consisted of Lieutenants Anthony Marsloe, Paul Alfieri, Joachim Titolo and the lesser-ranked Ensign James Murray. The small unit split into two teams of two — one embarking with the Americans at Licata and the other with the GIs who came on shore at Gela.

After the war, Alfieri explained how they had planned to contact immigrants who had been deported back to their homeland from the US after committing a crime. It was in Licata that this strategy came to fruition. Alfieri used his connection with a local *mafioso* to gain entry to the building which housed the Italian naval command. It was not American forces but a raggle-taggle bunch of local gunmen who stormed the headquarters, killing the German guards. Lieutenant Alfieri then blew the door off the safe inside, thereby discovering plans detailing the island's defences, a stack of radio codebooks and maps of minefields dotted throughout the Mediterranean.

This story would lead one to believe that the push towards Palermo was conducted hand in glove with the mafia. Real events, however, were far more complex and nuanced. Certain tales have been repeated so often that they have passed into the island's folklore and their veracity is seldom questioned. One story in particular centres on the central hilltop town of Villalba. Prior to the arrival of the American ground troops, it seems the central Piazza Madrice was buzzed on two occasions by a fighter plane which had a yellow flag attached to its tail. If legend is to be believed, the said flag sported a prominent black 'L'. The plane also dropped a package addressed to Uncle Calò, which included another yellow piece of fabric emblazoned with an 'L'.

When a scout group of American troops eventually arrived, the leading tank also carried the yellow standard. From inside the armoured vehicle, a Sicilian-American officer emerged and, using the local dialect, asked for Don Calò. Once he had made himself known, the Americans then invited Uncle Calò to accompany them. Don or Uncle Calò was in fact Calogero Vizzini, the *capo* mafia of the town who had an island-wide reputation. The 'L' on the flag stood for Lucky

Luciano, a Sicilian-American gangster born in Lercara Friddi who had been imprisoned in the US — the implication was that Luciano was collaborating with the American forces and was requesting the help and arms of his island brethren. The problem with this account is, as mafia expert John Dickie points out, that most historians consider it to be more fiction than fact. Having only been written down in 1962, the story is taken from an account by Michele Pantaleone, a left-wing politician and author who had had many justified run-ins with Vizzini.

Vizzini did go on to become the mayor of Villalba, irrespective of whether he had or had not spoken in detail to American forces at that moment and regardless of the yellow flag and other such elaborate embellishments. Furthermore it is impossible to deny that, from the other side of the Atlantic, Luciano was involved in the war effort. Long before the Americans reached Palermo and requisitioned The Palms, Naval Intelligence had been in contact with Lucky Luciano in his prison cell in Dannemora in upstate New York. The gaol was nicknamed 'Little Siberia' because of its freezing position near the Canadian border, but Luciano was to be moved closer to the Big Apple as he continued to co-operate with officialdom.

Details of mafia collusion with the navy's espionage branch can be found in the Herlands Report of 1954, an investigation instigated by Luciano's nemesis, the prosecutor Thomas E. Dewey. It focuses on organised crime's role in protecting the New York dockyards from infiltration by Fascist sympathisers. The Normandie, a liner being prepared for troop transport, caught fire and sank whilst docked in the city; enemy sabotage was suspected. This escalated the authorities' attempts at countering Axis infiltration, whether it came from American supporters of Fascism or from the landing of covert agents. During such a time of national crisis Lieutenant Marsloe, one of the intelligence officers who subsequently landed on the Sicilian beaches, was convinced of the need to obtain information from whatever source, no matter how dubious the credentials, even if it meant dealing with the criminal underworld. Luciano was charged with the task of helping naval intelligence set up a network of Italian-American informants working in the fishing industry who could alert the government to possible sabotage.

It is easier to demonstrate how American *mafiosi* lent their support to securing North American coasts than it is to verify the more nebulous connections they may have facilitated in Sicily itself when it came to helping troops in combat. Initially, as US forces moved across central Sicily towards Palermo, they required little in the way of such aid. The British, who had advanced along the east coast towards Messina, encountered much more resistance, especially from the German contingents they met who were retreating towards the Straits for an escape to the mainland. After fierce initial fighting, the US army often rolled into isolated central villages finding nothing but the smiling faces of locals relieved to be at the mercy of a more benign regime. GIs of Italian extraction would chat with the villagers and hand around the kind of treats Sicilian children would not have seen for years.

The commander of the US Seventh Army was General George Patton, nicknamed 'Old Blood and Guts'. Field Marshal Bernard Montgomery, the British commander, was expecting Patton to act as protection for the flank of his troops as they pushed inland from the coasts of Pachino and Avola. Patton, however, had other ideas and rather than stationing himself centrally, he persuaded the campaign leader, General Harold Alexander, to allow him to take Palermo. Strategically, this made little sense as the capital is situated a considerable distance to the west of Messina where all the action was taking place, however Patton saw Palermo in propagandist terms; he knew the occupation of Sicily's capital would make a good news story.

When General Patton's army entered Palermo on 22 July 1943, the people took to the streets. Throngs, many rows deep, lined the roads — some Palermitani even brandished banners of welcome. A black and white grainy image taken on the day shows a poster proclaiming '*Le nazioni unite*'. By way of elaboration, its words of hurt — '*dopo venti anni di ogni sorta di angherie e di soprisi*' ('after twenty years of all kinds of harassment and arrogance') — are salved by the final line which celebrates '*l'ora della desiderata libertà*' ('the time of longed-for freedom').

Patton, riding in a motor convoy behind the initial troop contingent, was in a desperate hurry to reach the city and proclaim its liberation. His jeep, proudly displaying the three-star pennant of his rank, came to a grinding halt in an unlikely traffic jam on a Sicilian mountain road. It seems the hold-up was due to a stubborn mule pulling a cart painted in the island's traditional bright colours. Patton drove to the head of the convoy and, a few minutes later, traffic started to move freely. As the soldiers passed the point where the mule had refused to budge, they saw the animal lying dead at the bottom of a ravine and the cart smashed to pieces. The short-tempered Patton had berated the peasant owner and ordered a minion to shoot the obstinate beast. In a moment the job was done and the wooden wagon destroyed. Nobody was going to spoil Patton's moment of glory.

As befitting this rather self-aggrandising capture of a city with no strategic value, General Patton commandeered the most lavish hotel, The Palms, as his bed and breakfast whilst setting up headquarters in the Palazzo dei Normanni. Undoubtedly, the recapture of Palermo would eventually have been a part of the Allied invasion, but Old Blood and Guts wanted it now and wanted the best it had to offer. It is not difficult to imagine his self-assured, dominant presence confidently striding through the hotel foyer, whilst staff obsequiously obeyed his barked orders. As it transpired, his residence at The Palms was short-lived. A few days later, leaving a skeleton military command behind, he turned his attention to Messina. Leading his troops along the Tyrrhenian coast, he orchestrated an amphibious landing which resulted in the capture of the city before the battle-weary British and Canadians were able to arrive.

Although Patton beat his rival, Montgomery, to Messina, he would have reached the city more quickly had he not been distracted by Palermo. A German Panzer division had landed on the northern coast, thereby providing more resistance than he would have previously encountered. In fact, Operation Husky was considered in some quarters something of a failure despite the victorious outcome. The Germans were able to evacuate, according to official figures, 39,569 men, 9,605 vehicles and over 2,000 tonnes of ammunition and fuel; in fact, General von Senger described the operation as 'a glorious retreat'. The Italians also managed to evacuate a considerable number of troops; although, with the fall of Mussolini, they would take little part in the remainder of the war.

Having taken the island, the Allies were now charged with its governance and administration. Major General Rennell, an English aristocrat, was appointed as head of AMGOT (Allied Military Government for Occupied Territories). The island was split into areas administered by a SCAO (Senior Civil Affairs Officer) — the SCAO for Palermo and its surroundings was the American Lieutenant Colonel Charles Poletti (1903–2002) who chose The Palms as his base of operations. Poletti was a multilingual son of Italian immigrants, who had studied at Harvard and the University of Rome. He was a trained lawyer and subsequently a politician, becoming the 46th governor of New York in 1942, albeit for just one month.

Whispers of controversy have long surrounded Poletti's tenure as Civil Affairs Officer in Palermo, most of which are mere hearsay. It is often repeated that Vito Genovese, the notorious American mobster who had been born near Naples, acted as his driver and interpreter. Naturally, Poletti always refuted this claim — and, to be fair, his counter-argument made the solid assertion that he had no need of such services given his fluency in Italian. It is true that the exiled Genovese pursued many black-market activities, but the majority of these were conducted from his base in Nola, a town some thirty kilometres outside Naples.

Poletti and his senior, Lord Rennell, faced a very complicated situation in trying to stabilise Sicilian governance. From his room in the hotel the problems faced by the citizens of Palermo would have been all too obvious to the former Governor of New York. The city had been heavily bombed by the Allies with the extensive damage evident from Via Roma. Many people were homeless, demobbed soldiers roamed the streets in search of gainful employment and food shortages were plaguing an already malnourished population. In short, the conditions for a surge in crime were perfect.

The SCAOs had to strip away the layers of Fascist administration and replace them with a civil service untainted by the years of Mussolini's rule. When an AMGOT representative arrived at a town hall, he had to think on his feet and make decisions on the spur of the moment that often had lasting consequences. Many *mafiosi* had solid anti-Fascist credentials and were quick to push themselves forward when the Allies were casting round for someone new to appoint as a mayor or councillor.

Sometimes, the appointment was made with knowing complicity and sometimes with simplistic naivety. Poletti was aware of what he called a lot of 'free-wheeling on [the] part of officers of AMGOT'. He correctly noted that 'confusion, misunderstanding and dispersion of responsibility will result'. He wanted greater decentralisation of powers hitherto based in Rome.

One of the greatest criticisms aimed at Charles Poletti was his connection with the kind of Sicilian separatists who would have welcomed his desire for a degree of self-rule, seeing it as the gateway to independence. Lucio Tasca (1880–1957), son of Giuseppe (see chapter 2), was a leading figure in the movement that quickly formed to promote Sicilian separatism. Tasca and the Duchess of Cesaro visited Poletti at The Palms and invited him to dine at the restaurant. The trump card played by the wily Tasca was his ability to present himself as an opponent of Mussolini. Perhaps falling into the same trap as the free-wheelers he had previously condemned, Poletti was happy to see Tasca appointed as Mayor of Palermo. Lord Rennell was less happy with the new incumbent and saw clearly enough the repercussions of Tasca's elevated position. He understood that separatism was, at the time, inextricably linked to the mafia and that the incoming mayor had some very dubious friends. He would take no part in the convivial dinners where the Nero d'Avola flowed freely.

The separatist movement created a rift between the Allies, with the Americans thinking the British were encouraging such notions and the British laying the blame at the Americans' door. Tim Newark, in *The Mafia at War*, quotes from a British Foreign Office memorandum written by Harold Swan, the Consul-General based in Naples, which states that the landed gentry, who supported independence, had thrown their lot in with the mafia. The criminal organisation sensed an opportunity to forge the island in its own image. Swan felt that Poletti, unwittingly or otherwise, was encouraging the burgeoning desire for separation and he had a point; in fact, a letter exists from Tasca to Poletti, in which the former thanks his dear friend for all his assistance and help.

As rich separatists dined with AMGOT representatives, the state of the island was becoming perilous. In Palermo alone, the murder rate virtually trebled and the number of burglaries increased six-fold. The old spectre of banditry arose once again — late night travel was inadvisable, especially if carrying any luggage of value. Two decisions were made: one, rather controversially, involved the strengthening of the *carabinieri*, and the other, rather bizarrely, saw London 'bobbies' pounding the beat outside the Liberty-style entrance to The Palms. The officers were seconded from the Metropolitan Police and were asked to perform all manner of tasks from straightforward administration to the monitoring of the Italian police. Tim Newark tells us that one of the officers quipped that AMGOT really stood for 'Aged Military Gentlemen on Tour', given that the majority of the policemen were closer to retirement than initial recruitment.

If this vignette has a faint whiff of *Dads' Army*, some of the stories that emerge from this era are more serious. In his book, *The Mafia and the Allies*, Ezio Costanzo mentions an OSS (Office of Strategic Services) report that accuses Poletti of readmitting former Fascists to the police force. It makes the damning allegation that he 'does not understand the situation in Sicily, its population or the forces at work within local politics'. Poletti would undoubtedly have countered with the claim that the *carabinieri* were best placed to understand the criminal world they faced and that reconstructing a police force from scratch was not a viable option.

Sicily was not unusual in having a wartime black market; the figure of the spiv has consistently featured in British films set during this period of conflict, but Sicily's particular circumstances made the illegal trading of rationed goods a godsend for the mafia. AMGOT did not only rely on the Met, they also turned to special investigators who had experience in the worst aspects of North American racketeering. Newspaper reports began to circulate in America that once again raised the spectre of the mafia as a dangerous phenomenon. Some even expressed surprise that organised crime had made a reappearance after the repressions of Cesare Mori (see chapter 3).

Poletti actively encouraged the rearming of the *carabinieri*, even if weapons were carried by men who had once supported Mussolini. To ensure standards of policing were appropriate, these men often had shadows — the aforementioned bobbies or even the military police.

Poletti's rationale was simply that he thought the populace would not respect the forces of law and order if they did not carry guns. Despite such reinforcements, the Allies would never redirect too many military personnel in the chasing of criminals — they still had a war to win. Evidence of the woeful under-resourcing of the police could be seen by the beginning of December 1943, when major demonstrations and disturbances broke out across the island's large conurbations, especially in Palermo. At their heart were the usual complaints surrounding rationing and the inequitable distribution of food but, more alarmingly for AMGOT, these complaints were driven by political forces, particularly Communism, the rise of which disturbed Poletti and his fellow civil officers.

The separatists were fervently anti-Communist, a stance that pushed them further into the arms of certain AMGOT representatives, despite the official policy that all political activity should be avoided as far as possible. American Military Intelligence Officer Captain W.E. Scotten, a former Vice-Consul in Palermo, wrote a report that recognised the political dangers of over-reliance on certain factions and the complications of having the mafia as part of the mix. He alleged that eighty per cent of appointments made by Allied Civil Officers were given to those who had separatist leanings. The waters were becoming so muddied that Allied officials found it nearly impossible to establish a clear picture.

This was not the case with Joseph Russo, an American OSS agent stationed in Palermo whose father hailed from Corleone. More than one book on the subject of AMGOT quotes Russo's 1993 BBC TV interview in which he admits to actively seeking out the criminal element:

> When I got to Sicily and took over, the first thing I did I started looking for the *malavita* — the criminals — and it turned out they were mostly Mafiosi. They liked my name and the fact that my father was born in Corleone... I got to know these people — the high Mafiosi — and they were big. They got to be real big. It didn't take them long to re-cement their solidarity...

Ezio Costanzo even claims that Russo met these bosses monthly and valued their inside information. Costanzo enumerates a litany of jobs offered to *mafiosi* that would have provided them with diversification opportunities with no questions asked. These included roles such as interpreter, warehouse operative, harvest administrator and, of course, mayor. In the same BBC interview, Russo laid the responsibility for the appointment of *mafiosi* to important positions squarely at the door of Charles Poletti, a claim that Poletti always refuted, just as he had denied Genovese's presence as his interpreter.

Costanzo asserts that Poletti held parties and working meetings at The Palms for 'mysterious characters connected to organised crime'. It is not clear who these 'characters' may have been, or whether they visited Poletti in the guise of people who supported the politics of independence. We have not been able to find tangible accounts of these meetings but have discovered descriptions of the hotel during this time. Having been commandeered as a centre for operations, some of the building's more extravagant elements were gradually stripped back to accommodate the needs of administration. Plush furnishings, expensive carpets, velvet drapes and Art Deco ornaments were put into storage, replaced by more functional and sober items befitting a country under military occupation.

When Poletti was meeting the aristocratic Lucio Tasca to discuss matters of separatist politics, he was also in contact with Andrea Finocchiaro Aprile (1878–1964). Aprile had been an Under-Secretary of State in the era prior to Fascism and was at the head of a faction that preferred a complete schism between Sicily and the Italian mainland. His leadership was favoured by the landed gentry and organised crime. Like many espousing the taking back of control from a wider power, his rhetoric was full of vague promises and exaggerated sunny uplands, only attainable through his version of independence. He was profuse in his criticism of anyone who stood in his way, whether they were monarchists, Communists or the Allies themselves.

In Corleone in January 1944, he rose to his feet and gave a speech boasting of how Sicilian-Americans would persuade their government to back independence whilst casually name-dropping Anthony Eden as a man who understood the average Sicilian's desire for separatism. This was the latest of many such speeches and Poletti must have regretted his part in letting the separatist genie out of the bottle. Later, in a meeting held in Bagheria, Aprile even admitted to being a friend of the mafia, whilst maintaining his abhorrence of violence. It became apparent that Aprile's oratory bombast, together with increased poverty, was leading to riots, which had started in October of the previous year when Italian soldiers had turned their weapons on a crowd storming the Palermo Prefecture resulting in 162 casualties.

Traces of this era of conflict are still visible today in the urban fabric of Palermo. This may not include the bullet holes from the weapons discharged in October 1943 but is evident in the occasional ruined building in the Kalsa district. Conventional wisdom places the blame on the mafia, and this has a degree of veracity, but not in the way that many would expect. Wearing his anti-racket hat, Poletti put a stop to demolition contracts after a few months of AMGOT rule. Costanzo tells us that the newspaper *Sicilia Liberata*, begun by the Allies to keep the local populace informed, had reported that a gang were cornering the market in falsely over-recording the amount of rubble to be removed, whilst threatening the civil engineers who needed to accurately report on the work. Many of the demolition contracts were never reinstated, but this paled into insignificance compared with the so-called 'Sack of Palermo', the construction boom that began in the 1950s which saw a concrete blanket descend on the Conca d'Oro.

The quagmire faced by AMGOT — a mix of rationing, the breakdown of law and order, political in-fighting and the rush to fill a power vacuum — must have contributed to the Allied powers' overwhelming desire to pass the government of Sicily back to native authorities. On 11 February 1944 overall control was returned to the Italian government, although the Allies maintained a strong presence through the ACC (Allied Control Commission). Francesco Musotto became the governor of Sicily; he was Poletti's favoured candidate and not from Finocchiaro Aprile's party. Tim Newark suggests, via the evidence of an OSS report, that Sicilians were not impressed with Musotto who had been a lawyer engaged in defending mafia clients during the Mussolini era.

The change of government had a negligible impact on the problems faced by the island. By the end of 1944, Sicilian High Commissioner Salvatore Aldisio was still talking about the link between the mafia and separatists, adding the extra component of vagabond banditry to this fusion of forces. The most famous of all Sicilian bandits during the post-invasion era was Salvatore Giuliano (1922–50), a handsome and charismatic young man from Montelepre, a small town twenty-seven kilometres to the west of Palermo. His life on the run started in September 1943 when he was stopped by the *carabinieri* and two *guardie campestri*, who wanted to see his ID card and then demanded information regarding the grain he was carrying. Giuliano knew the black-market provenance of his load but refused to divulge the details, even under threat of violence. He was in no position to pay a bribe and understood that criminal charges would have a significant financial impact on his family.

Three of the men were distracted by the arrival of a second mule and its owner. Giuliano was left with one of the *carabinieri*, and then witnessed the three officials of the law take money from the mule owner. Enraged and feeling as though he had no option, Giuliano knocked the gun from the hand of the remaining *carabiniere* and made a run for it. Before he could disappear into a nearby thicket, he was fired upon and wounded. He took a gun from his sock and pulled the trigger, killing the officer nearest to him. In the confusion, the young man from Montelepre escaped to the hills, where others joined him, forming a band of thieves who styled themselves as latter-day Robin Hoods. As with all legends, the reality was far more complex.

It is true that some of the money and goods taken from the richer members of society were given to the poor, but it is also true that Giuliano needed the downtrodden of Montelepre and the surrounding districts to act as his shield and protection. When he descended from the hills, somebody had to accommodate him and remain silent regarding his whereabouts. As a counterbalance to the legend of altruistic robbery and kidnapping, John Dickie points out that Salvatore's band were ruthless in dealing with any betrayal, leaving a trail of corpses as evidence.

Throughout his reign as Sicily's most famous bandit, Giuliano was constantly seeking a form of redemption that would enable him to return to the family hearth. His father had spent time in America and, consequently, Salvatore looked fondly upon the American way of life, an outlook which made him a fervent anti-Communist. He was approached by the separatists to become an active part of the

Esercito volontario per l'indipendenza della Sicilia (Voluntary Army for Sicilian Independence). EVIS, as it was known, was intended to be the military wing of the political movement sympathetic to cessation, and its role was to attack the Italian state. Giuliano enthusiastically took to the job of waging war on the *carabinieri*. He saw an independent Sicily as his opportunity to return to his old life.

Giuliano even went to the unusual extreme of writing to the US President, Harry S. Truman. Gavin Maxwell, in his book, *God Protect Me from My Friends*, quotes the letter in full. The most pertinent section contains the following statement: 'We definitely do not intend to remain with a nation that considers Sicily a land to use when they need it and as something evil and diseased when they do not. For these reasons we wish to be joined to the United States of America.' It was a futile gesture from a man boxed into a corner who saw little other recourse. Many who have written on the subject believe that Giuliano could not have maintained his outlaw status for such a sustained period without the tacit support of the wilder fringes of the independence movement and its mafia friends.

However, to imagine that Giuliano was restricted to the caves, hills and friendly refuges of western Sicily would be a mistake. There is more than one report of his entering Palermo, and the oddest account comes from the pen of playwright Arthur Miller (1915–2005). Miller had struck up a friendship with Vincent Longhi, a lawyer running for Congress in 1948, who also had a sideline as a folk musician, playing with the likes of Woodie Guthrie and Leadbelly. Longhi had decided to travel to Calabria and Sicily in a bid to appeal to Italian-American voters and Miller happily tagged along. When the pair reached Palermo, they checked into The Palms.

Miller was disappointed with what he found, both inside and outside the hotel. His diary mentions the effects of the bombing on the city along with a vignette detailing the sparse interior of The Palms, further denuded of its decorative furnishing, in spite of the lingering glamour of the Art Deco architecture still intact after the harsh attentions of the US Airforce and several near misses during bombing raids. One missile had actually passed through the room of Baron Vincenzo Greco Militello, awakening the startled aristocrat but otherwise causing little damage. Longhi and Miller knew they would have to leave the hotel's confines to find a black-market meal worth eating. They happened upon a restaurant in a down-at-heel little square. Inside, they found a bizarre mix of clientele from bleached blonde wannabe starlets to Sicilian mamas in widows' weeds. Ages ranged from skinny adolescents to elderly intellectuals and professions from prostitute to doctor.

No sooner had they sat down than Longhi started to behave unnaturally, his face colouring profusely. Miller, in his autobiography *Timebends*, describes the scene in tragicomic tones. In response to Longhi's serious plea that under no circumstances should he turn around to see who was sitting behind him, Miller laughingly suggested it might be Mussolini. Longhi was unable to see the funny side, whispering to his friend that the diner causing him such consternation was none other than Lucky Luciano. Luciano had been released from gaol in America in 1946 and expelled to Italy. Contrary to the more outlandish speculations concerning Luciano's war effort, the gangster was not in Sicily during World War II and, if his sentence had been shortened at all, it was due to the aid he had given in protecting the eastern seaboard of the US. *The New York Times* reported he had been of some use with regard to Operation Husky but the article lacks detail. John Dickie says that Luciano's length of incarceration was customary, if not longer than usual, for the offence he had committed.

To make matters worse for Miller and Longhi, Luciano engaged the pair in conversation, suggesting they order what he was eating. He strolled over to their table and pulled up a chair. He was particularly intrigued to learn Vincent had an Italian surname and was familiar with Brooklyn, an area that had been Luciano's old stomping ground. The gangster's eye wandered to the case that Miller had placed on the floor by his seat — doubtless he was envisioning some form of weapon. As the conversation turned to its contents, the other diners had vanished, leaving the trio by themselves. Rather sheepishly, Miller handed the case, containing nothing more sinister than a camera, to the interested mobster. If Luciano was somewhat nonplussed by its innocence, he was even more surprised that the playwright and lawyer were touring in post-war Palermo.

Longhi explained his political mission whilst Miller obliquely observed Luciano's divided visage. The right side of his face was drawn downwards, in evil contrast to its more lively left-hand neighbour. At the end of the meal, the gangster offered to pay the bill, dropping a wedge of folded notes on the table without counting them. Much to Miller's horror, Luciano insisted that his bodyguard drive them back to the hotel and, to add to the pair's dismay, slipped into the back of the car next to Longhi. When the green Lancia pulled up outside The Palms, they all climbed out and headed for the reception. When Luciano saw Miller's key, he remarked that his own room was the one next door. Miller made the mistake of hastily getting into the lift before the ageing mobster and the silent ride to their floor must have felt like an eternity.

Semi-safely ensconced in their room, Longhi and Miller whispered their post-mortem of the evening's events. Longhi, all too aware of Luciano's reputation, feverishly imagined the gangster's impressions of their intention. Were they there to kill him as mob rivals? Or were they clandestine FBI agents looking for covert information on his criminal activities as an exile? Worry and exhaustion eventually compelled the two men to fall asleep. It was Longhi who was first awoken by a rap at the door, swiftly followed by a more insistent knock. Miller laughed at Longhi's heightened state of alert, prompting the pair to double over in silent hysterics.

After the third knock, Longhi opened the door to a handsome, striking young man in a blue cap and woollen plaid jacket. Despite shortages in petrol and a lack of cars to rent, the visitor, who had clearly been informed by Luciano of their desire to tour Sicily, offered to put a car at their disposal, refusing payment except for some American cigarettes. Ten years later, Miller was on an aeroplane seated next to the director Peter Brook. Brook was enthusing about a new movie project, showing the playwright clippings from various newspapers about a Sicilian bandit who had been gunned down some years previously. The director told Miller of the fame achieved by the bandit and his folkloric status that had charmed more than one female journalist. As Miller flicked through the pages, he came across a close-up of the dead outlaw's face. At that moment, his mind raced back to post-war Palermo and that insistent knock on his hotel room door. Miller believed that their generous visitor had been none other than Salvatore Giuliano.

That Giuliano could have obtained black market gasoline is plausible; that he would have been Luciano's gopher or have brazenly strolled into The Palms is less so. By 1948 the bandit's notoriety had taken an altogether darker turn, owing to an incident on one fateful day in 1947. It was May Day and families of a Communist persuasion had gathered at Portella della Ginestra, situated between the towns of Piana degli Albanesi and San Giuseppe Jato. The celebratory picnic was suddenly and brutally interrupted by indiscriminate gunfire coming from the surrounding hillside. Eleven people died, including children, and many were wounded. Giuliano and his band had carried out the attack which he said had initially been a plan to capture and execute Li Causi, the Communist Senator; he claimed that he had ordered his men to fire over the heads of the crowd. Li Causi was not in attendance and the supposed blow for separatism backfired as the wider Italian public were horrified by the massacre.

The incident did little for the already dwindling support for separatism. Out of the tangle of competing interests for political power in post-war Italy, the Christian Democrats were beginning to emerge as a force to be reckoned with. The 1947 constitution had given Sicily a degree of autonomy which took the sting from all but the most vociferous voices in the independence movement. Giuliano's usefulness to those wishing to wield political power had almost run its course. In 1950 he was found dead, sprawled in the courtyard of a house in Castelvetrano close to the southern coast of the island. The circumstances surrounding his death are still unclear; the official story has him being shot by the *carabinieri*, although many believe it was his cousin and second-in-command, Gaspare Pisciotta, who fired the fatal bullets in collusion with the police and other powers. Pisciotta mysteriously died in prison before he could reveal the truth.

Giuliano's gang may have been the last of Sicily's famous bandit outlaws, but the organisation that tolerated its existence showed no signs of demise; the mafia continued to spread its roots through the nascent and fragile democracy established on the island. Contacts with North American mobsters were now even easier after the likes of Lucky Luciano had been exiled to Italy. Luciano did not stay in Sicily and moved to Naples, although he always maintained close contact with the land of his forefathers. Often under surveillance by the authorities, his passport was revoked in 1952 and two years later he was placed under curfew at home which lasted a few more years. These actions were prompted by suspicions of his involvement in the drugs trade.

Miller and Longhi had good reason to be wary of Luciano at The Palms in the light of this report (uncovered by Tim Newark) from the British Consulate in Palermo during his first stay in the city: '... I am told, on good authority, that some of the leading members of the Mafia have called on him at the hotel on more than one occasion.' In 1957 The Palms would come into even sharper focus when it was used as the venue for a momentous meeting for organised crime. The backdrop to this infamous gathering was a burgeoning trade in narcotic smuggling and the post-war sack of Palermo. Having infiltrated the construction business and cultivated connections with the ruling Christian Democrats, the mafia had taken control of building projects in the city. Districts of innate natural beauty and elegant Baroque architectural design were in the process of being swept aside as concrete towers started to populate the landscape on the outskirts of the city. Furthermore, the Sicilian mafia and their North American brethren had their sights set on dominating the international heroin trade, using Palermo as the major transportation hub on the route to America.

A central figure at the meeting was Giuseppe Bonanno, nicknamed 'Joe Bananas' by the American press. He had been born in Castellammare del Golfo, just over an hour's drive west along the coast from Palermo. Bonanno had left for America during the dictatorship of Benito Mussolini and had been involved in the internecine struggles for the control of organised crime in certain districts of New York, ending up as one of the five bosses of the New York mafia families. Ostensibly on holiday in Sicily in 1957, Bonanno toured the sites, visiting his former home, the nearby ancient temple of Segesta and places of interest in the city itself. The actual meetings at the hotel are shrouded in mystery — even the principal room given over to discussion is up for debate. Some authors have placed the mobsters in the Blue Room (Sala Azzura), with its appropriately azure papered walls and rich gold cornicing; others have suggested the heavily embossed style and marbled flooring of the

Sala Wagner. It is probably just as likely that the men visited each other in their suites.

John Dickie in his history of the Sicilian mafia, *Cosa Nostra*, dates the gathering to October of that year and recounts that it lasted four days. Unsurprisingly, a comprehensive list of attendees will never be available, but Dickie details participants from the US, naturally those from the Bonanno crime family, and Sicilians including the head of the Castellammare del Golfo family and Giuseppe Genco Russo, the *mafioso* who had close wartime connections with Calogero Vizzini. Lucky Luciano seemingly also made an appearance, taking a trip down to Palermo from Naples.

The story of the 'conference' is often portrayed as an overarching deal between organised crime on both sides of the Atlantic; in reality, it brought together, under one roof, those gangsters who felt connected by their heritage and blood. Despite the surveillance of characters such as Luciano, the police paid scant attention to the powerful gathering. Given the increase in heroin trafficking after 1957, hindsight tells us that it should have been higher on their list of priorities.

Watching from the wings was a curious character, impeccably dressed, a Havana cigar hanging from his lips, who, by the time of the meeting, had already been resident at The Palms for ten years or more. To tell his story, we firstly have to head south for the town of Castelvetrano. Although some have questioned his aristocratic status, we will give this character the title by which he was universally known, Baron Giuseppe Di Stefano. His Baronetcy was supposedly linked to the town of Sciacca, but his lands were just to the north of Castelvetrano. How Di Stefano (1906–98) came to live as a permanent resident in The Palms is, like so many Sicilian stories, a patchwork frayed at the edges.

Di Stefano's estate was a mixture of citrus and almond cultivation, olive groves and wide stretches of scrubland, ideal for hunting. In this respect, he was a landed gentleman typical of many from this region. A 1995 article in the weekly magazine *Famiglia Cristiana* claimed that Di Stefano had inherited his wealth from an aunt, an assertion backed up by the one-time mayor of Castelvetrano and former senator, Giuseppe Bongiorno. If we imagine a man having just turned forty, strolling amongst the almond trees on his estate, we would likely picture a well-dressed squire carrying a hunting shotgun, its barrel unhinged across his arm, perhaps a faithful dog at his heel. Suddenly, Di Stefano sees movement amongst the trees, where a clandestine figure appears to be picking the fresh produce from the branches. Instinctively, he loads the gun and snaps the barrel shut, taking aim at the interloper on his land — he may never have meant to kill him.

One shot was enough to fell the youth who had the kind of mafia connections that made the Baron wish he had never pulled the trigger — at least this is one version of the story that leads to Di Stefano's exile in the palatial confines of The Palms. Another account involves a car and the same youth who absentmindedly strays into the path of the speeding aristocrat; yet another story distorts the first, seeing the young man cruelly kicked by the Baron for stealing his almonds in place of being shot. The youth subsequently expires from his injuries. In all these versions the problem — aside from the obvious fact that the young man dies — concerns the deceased's connections to the mafia. Usually, blood would wash blood to maintain honour, but the Baron seemingly escaped such a death sentence. Whether this was through wealth and aristocratic connections or, as some have speculated, his own association with organised crime, the story has Giuseppe Di Stefano's sentence commuted to life inside the hotel's gilded cage.

What was the Baron's own explanation for the unusual decision to spend over half his life as a hotel guest? For some kind of answer, we turn to Toti Librizzi, the renowned barman of The Palms' Gattopardo Bar. Librizzi knew Di Stefano better than most and reports that the Baron was clipped in his responses to those who dared to ask the dreaded question regarding mafia involvement in his exile. His favoured repost was '*Sono favole*' ('They are tall tales'). Although Librizzi feels that the real reason will never be known, he is at pains to point out that the Baron was a good and generous man who attracted many well-known friends, taking meals with some of the brightest and best in the fields of show business, art and science. The barman's celebrity revelations and Di Stefano's friendship with the *beau monde* will feature in subsequent chapters.

Librizzi's first encounter with the Baron reveals the reverence in which the hotel staff held their esteemed guest. On the fourth floor of the building there was a terrace that had come to be known as the roof garden. Drawn to the greenery, the newly employed barman saw a man in shorts with swept-back thinning hair attending to the lemons, jasmine, cactuses and hibiscus. Unaware of his identity, the barman complimented him on his care of the plants. Di Stefano responded with the offer of a coffee, which Librizzi parried with his own offer of an espresso. The barman was somewhat shaken when, on reporting to colleagues his meeting with 'the gardener', they told him in hushed tones that this was the Baron, and could not believe that he had summoned the temerity to address Di Stefano so casually.

When the pair met again, Librizzi was far more obsequious in his language — a move understood by Di Stefano who, years later, confided to the barman that he had appreciated the spontaneity of their first meeting. For the Baron, Librizzi would always be 'Totino', the man who never asked awkward questions and was ready with a smile and a greeting. Like many bar staff in prestigious establishments, Librizzi was in a unique position to observe the comings and goings of the guests. The website of the foundation *Il Giardino di Colapesce*, established by Librizzi after his retirement, refutes the hearsay that Di Stefano never left the interior of The Palms.

During the 1970s, the aristocrat would escape for short stays in Naples where he could indulge his love of opera at the Teatro San Carlo. There were also rumours that he kept a mistress in the city, but her identity has never been revealed. It is also true that during the later years of his stay, Di Stefano would spend part of August at the Villa Igiea — that other Basile masterpiece transformed into a hotel. If the mafia did have a *fatwah* on his head, it seems they had somewhat relaxed their surveillance after he had spent so many years of comfortable incarceration behind the Liberty doors of The Palms. The Baron even took the extreme measure of affording himself a walk after lunch, slipping into Via Roma and along Via Wagner before returning by way of Via Principe di Granatelli.

The Baron's unusual lifestyle has been a gift for writers who have either fictionalised his story or attempted to piece together the facts in documentary accounts. Among those who have sprinkled fact with fiction is Philippe Fusaro, the French son of Pugliese parents, in his novel *Palermo solo*. Many journalists have been fascinated by the mystery surrounding his supposed house arrest, including Gaetano Basile who gave space to the story in his book, *Palermo è...* Sebastián Montero Sánchez even co-opts little Rosalia Lombardo, the embalmed child entombed in the Capuchin Monastery, to relate Di Stefano's complex tale in the book *El Barón y la niña eternal* (*The Baron and the Eternal Girl*).

Fusaro accurately portrays the Baron's daily routine which gave structure to an otherwise rudderless existence. Each morning would see a visit from the barber who would come up from the Kalsa district and, according to Fusaro, knock three times on the suite door before entering and shaving the aristocrat's well-proportioned visage. Di Stefano would sit in a leather chair by the window overlooking Via Roma, and lean his neck backwards into the headrest, vulnerable but without fear. His meals were not those that would be served to the other guests at the hotel; instead, he would have his favourite chef, Paolo Sciacca, prepare something to order, often incorporating fresh produce that he had requested from his land in Castelvetrano or fish, caught that day, from the port of Mazara del Vallo. Apparently, the Baron was so fond of garlic that the pungent fumes of his breath would warn of his imminent arrival.

Di Stefano abhorred any form of mass media; he refused to read the papers and reacted to the arrival of television at The Palms with patrician distaste. He received his news from the chef who would give him the edited highlights on a daily basis, doubtless a mixture of local gossip and national politics. His meals were taken at the '*tavolo del barone*', that is to say, the table set aside for him in the restaurant (La Palmetta) which afforded him views of each corner of the room. Prior to placing himself on public display, in the earlier years of his stay it is said that he only had his food delivered via room service.

One of the biggest blows suffered by Di Stefano during his sojourn was the closure of his beloved roof terrace. The hotel management wanted to commandeer the space for what we would now describe as networking events. By way of compensation, the director agreed to amalgamate two suites, thereby creating number 204 — the suite of rooms always associated with Di Stefano. He was able to populate the enlarged space with his favourite plants and tend to them each day.

All the Baron's financial needs were covered by a man from the Banco di Sicilia who would pay a personal visit to the hotel. His sartorial requirements were met by a visiting tailor instructed to take measurements and then deliver the fabricated item at a later date. Di Stefano would only invest trust in those people he saw on a regular basis and who provided him with the precise services he had requested. He also had a favourite amongst the hotel waiting staff, Giacomo Maniscalco — the only member of The Palms' personnel to receive a bequest in his will, namely his shoes and linen suits.

Clearly, the Baron was a creature of habit, and further evidence of this can be seen in his yearly clandestine trip to Castelvetrano every November. Librizzi, the barman, informs us that a driver would collect the Baron at 2 a.m. and drive him to the cemetery where his parents were buried. He would lay flowers on their graves and return to the hotel, arriving back no later than 5 a.m. Presumably, these quiet hours before dawn allowed him the privacy he required. However, the nature of these visits can be contrasted with eye-witness accounts from the early 1950s. Vito Marino of *Castelvetrano News* can recall seeing him in the town during this period when he was supposedly restricted to the hotel's confines.

Marino remembers him striding through the streets, his head held high with his brilliantined hair catching the light. During the cooler hours of the burning summer, he would sit by the grandiose front door of his palazzo trying to catch a breath of fresh air. Apart from these dog days and the grape harvest, when he would supervise the unloading of the carts, Di Stefano was not to be seen. Just when you think you have a clear picture of the Baron's enigmatic life, these glimpses of the man on his home turf, however brief, send disturbing ripples through the water.

Gaetano Basile is one of the journalists who remains unconvinced of Giuseppe Di Stefano's patrician pedigree. He undertook an investigation that was adapted by Japanese television and turned into a screenplay, actually filmed at the hotel. Basile makes the claim that his choice to live as a perpetual guest was self-inflicted and merely a way of enjoying his wealth and power at the heart of Sicily's capital. Stripping away the eccentricities and stories of habitual obfuscation, there remain vestiges of possible criminal association. Nonetheless, Librizzi was aware of only two friendships with people he felt exuded the '*odore di mafia*', namely the Italian-Americans Giacinto Di Simone and Charles Orlando. Orlando was under suspicion by the Federal Bureau of Narcotics of having used his olive oil and cheese importing business to mask quantities of heroin being brought into the US.

In 1965 Orlando was arrested at The Palms; his reaction had the typical *sang-froid* of a man belittling his own fate. He requested that the police take him as quietly as possible, so as not to disturb the guests in the surrounding suites whom he claimed were good people. We are unaware of the room inhabited by Orlando, but we wonder if Di Stefano was tending his plants nearby. In 1966 *The New York Times* reported that Charles Orlando was petitioning to have his name cleared by the Italian courts.

It is more favourable to remember the self-exiled aristocrat as a great lover of music, one aspect of his life that is an irrefutable fact. When opera premieres were held at the Teatro Massimo and its smaller cousin, the Politeama, Di Stefano liked nothing better than to throw a party for the artists involved. A salon in The Palms would be set aside for this private affair and food dear to the Baron's heart would be sent from Castelvetrano, including delicate pastries from his favourite bakery. The elegant gathering is reminiscent of scenes in Visconti's 1963 film, *The Leopard*, where those selected from the cream of society would discuss matters of the day.

The Baron was a close friend of Giuseppe Di Stefano — no relation, but uncannily bearing the same name. The tenor, Giuseppe, was known as the 'Golden voice' and performed regularly through the decades from the 1940s until the 1990s. Both Luciano Pavarotti and José Carreras are on record as describing Di Stefano as their inspiration. In the 1950s, Di Stefano recorded a series of popular Italian operas for EMI with the equally lauded and famous Maria Callas. Both singers would stay at The Palms when working in Palermo and both would be guests of the Baron.

After more than fifty years of luxurious confinement, whatever the explanation behind it, the Baron had reached the venerable age of ninety-two. Even his medical care was provided by itinerant nurses who attended him at his request. During the Easter celebrations of 1998, the faithful Librizzi explains that they had prepared roast kid and the

traditional dessert of *cassata*, but Di Stefano was not to taste this final
meal, dying in his sleep. Contrary to the practice of most hotels, his body
was not removed via the staff corridors, leaving by the back entrance
next to the rubbish bins, but was accorded the honour of being carried,
ceremoniously, through the ornate foyer. Some say that he had asked his
faithful waiter, Giacomo, to cover his face with a large handkerchief in
order to mask his features from his enemies, even in death. The Baron's
body was cremated at Santa Maria dei Rotoli to the north of Villa Igiea
along the Tyrrhenian coast towards Mondello.

From his eyrie in suite 204, Di Stefano would have seen Palermo's
progression from post-war privation to its dubious overdevelopment in
the era of concrete. Hand in hand with this unrestrained urban sprawl
came the city's role as an *entrepôt* for hard drugs. The 1957 meeting of
mafiosi had obviously been intended as a way to orchestrate this trade;
however, life beyond the rule of law takes on its own momentum. Soon,
the amount of money to be made in the drug trade had rival factions
eyeing the prize. The early 1960s saw a spate of shootings, bombings
and retaliatory violence erupt on the streets of Palermo — it was met
with hysterical newspaper headlines. Mafia historian John Dickie says it
all started when a drug deal went bad and certain parties were short-
changed in their share of the final product.

Palermo was now a far cry from its *fin de siècle* self; some neighbourhoods had changed out of all recognition. The famous example
that typifies this wholesale destruction is that of Villa Deliella, another
stile Liberty building of Ernesto Basile design situated in Piazza Croci. Its
construction began in 1898 for the Deliella family who were related to
the powerful Lanza Brancifortes. The building was recognisable by its
hexagonal tower, capped with a spiked roof, with an ostentatious palm
softening the lines of the architecture.

Despite having been initially protected in 1954 as a building of
significance owing to its *stile Liberty* origins, the protection was
rescinded thanks to the fact that less than fifty years had passed since
its completion. This loophole allowed those behind the 1959 town
plan to push through permission for the destruction of the building.
On the afternoon of 28 November that year demolition began, and
those waking to croissants and coffee the following morning would

have been aghast at the gap in the skyline. By the end of the day, Villa Deliella had almost completely disappeared. The town plan was riddled with amendments, petitions and variations leading the first Antimafia Commission to declare that 'the administrative management of Palermo City Council reached unprecedented heights of deliberate non-observation of the law around 1960'.

At the height of what came to be known as the First Mafia War, Palermo was also attracting the attention of film directors, already enamoured with the glamour of Rome, and looking for further filming locations. The 1960 film *La Dolce Vita*, 'the sweet life' of Rome, became such a phenomenon that it was impossible for Italy's provincial centres to avoid pleasurable contamination by association. It was a change for reporters to focus on the visit of a starlet as opposed to the calculations of the mafia, whose worst excesses in the aforementioned war culminated in the 1963 Ciaculli car bomb massacre — an attempt on the life of *capo mafioso*, Salvatore Greco, thought to be present at the 1957 meeting at The Palms. Greco was unharmed, but the bomb killed four *carabinieri*, a police officer and the two army engineers sent to diffuse it.

In many ways, this explosion had a similar impact to the fateful assassination of Judge Giovanni Falcone in 1992, and the killing of his colleague Paolo Borsellino a few months later (see chapter 6). As with the events of 1992, the Ciaculli bomb brought the mafia to the wider attention of the Italian public as an organisation that could not only put in harm's way the forces of law and order, but also innocent bystanders. It made headline news throughout the country as journalists tried to think of a similar atrocity with which to compare it — inevitably the name Giuliano and the location Portella della Ginestra came to mind. The news would even have reached the ears of Baron Di Stefano, filtered through the colourful lens of his chef's daily reports.

5

LA DOLCE VITA

In 1954, as Palermo raced towards a self-destructive modernity, a man from another era sat at his desk in Via Butera crafting, in miniscule handwriting, his only significant contribution to the world of literature. The man in question favoured a thin moustache, emulating that of his ancestors. His habitual attire was a woollen suit, often worn with a waistcoat despite the island's punishing heat. The final flourish would be either a patterned bow tie or a simple tie but rarely an open-necked shirt. This disciplined apparel reflected both his aristocratic origins and his resolutely old-fashioned outlook.

We are, of course, referring to Giuseppe Tomasi di Lampedusa (1896–1957), author of *Il Gattopardo* (*The Leopard*). Lampedusa was the last in a long family line of Sicilian nobles whose ancestry can with certainty be traced back to twelfth-century Tuscany and perhaps even further to the Imperial Guard of Tiberius. Like so many of his class, Lampedusa did not have to earn a living but was able to follow his passions in life. A man of few words, painfully shy and content in the company of selected close friends, he preferred to immerse himself in literature. In the hours of his everyday solitude, he would read avidly, eventually deciding to impart some of his knowledge to those in his intimate literary circle including Francesco Orlando, who would later become a critic and essayist and Gioacchino Lanza, the young cousin he would eventually adopt as his son.

It was a trip to San Pellegrino Terme in northern Italy during the spring of 1954 that finally kick-started Lampedusa's latent desire to write for public consumption. His cousin, the poet Lucio Piccolo, had been invited to San Pellegrino for a literary conference and took

Lampedusa along for moral support. Piccolo was presented as a protégé of the poet and writer Eugenio Montale despite the fact that he was of a similar age. Lampedusa, realising that his cousin could make an impact irrespective of his advancing years, decided to put pen to paper himself.

The process of completing *The Leopard* was rather laboured. David Gilmour, in his biography *The Last Leopard*, points out that Lampedusa was as used to writing in French as he was in Italian. When his Latvian wife, Licy, was on one of her frequent visits to the Baltic coast, he would always write to her in French, their shared language of choice. As Gilmour notes, the fact he had to focus intently when writing in Italian may account for the carefully crafted phraseology and imagery present in the book. The majority of the text was either written at home in Via Butera or at the Caffè Mazzara off Via Ruggiero Settimo, a rather odd choice, given the plain concrete exterior of the building. Sadly, the Mazzara has recently closed its doors forever.

Two years later, at the start of 1956, Lampedusa was still struggling with his novel. The fifty-nine-year-old aristocrat had sidelined the text by dabbling with an autobiography which he was never to finish but, realising the importance of his *Leopard*, he once again refocussed and completed the work in March of that year. It was Francesco Orlando who turned Giuseppe's tightly-written lines into a typescript fit for submission to a publisher. Italy was then in the grip of neo-realism, a genre epitomised by Vittorio De Sica's film *Ladri di biciclette* (*Bicycle Thieves*), in which an impoverished father is forced to steal in an attempt to feed his family. The gap between Lampedusa's historical novel and the prevailing climate seemed unbridgeable.

After a rejection from the leading publishing house, Mondadori, Giuseppe added two more chapters but was still unable to persuade them to take on the text. Further rejections followed from Flaccovio and Einaudi before a revised typescript was accepted by Feltrinelli. Sadly, Lampedusa did not live to see the publication of his novel or, indeed, to hear of its acceptance. Feltrinelli's editorial director Giorgio Bassani, himself famous for his Ferrara novels, was the book's champion and wrote the preface to the original edition. By 1959 *The Leopard* had achieved the highest acclaim by being awarded the prestigious Strega Prize.

At the heart of the novel is the Prince of Salina, a proud but jaded and time-worn aristocrat. Often referred to as Don Fabrizio, the character is based on Lampedusa's great-grandfather, although many acquainted with the author have seen Lampedusa's own resemblance to the Prince. The book is set during the Risorgimento at a time when the island's nobility have to choose between the Bourbon status quo and Garibaldi's new horizons. Prince Salina represents the tradition and morality of a fast-receding era, whereas his nephew Tancredi is excited by the opportunity that change could bring. However, despite the fact that these two family members are pulling in opposite directions, they both recognise the need for continuity if not the means of achieving it. This is crystallised in Tancredi's famous assertion that everything will have to change in order for it to stay the same.

Tancredi then falls for the charms of the beautiful Angelica, whose father is the proto-*mafioso*, Don Calogero. Forced to receive the *arriviste* interloper at his noble home, Donnafugata, Prince Salina is both horrified and amused when Calogero arrives for dinner dressed in a totally inappropriate frock coat. He may be ignorant of etiquette, but Calogero nevertheless has acquired much wealth through his money-lending enterprises, while his future son-in-law has the manners and lineage only dreamt of by a man who has dragged himself up from peasant stock. The joining of the two families through marriage is finally agreed upon.

Whilst at the summer residence of Donnafugata, Prince Salina meets Chevalley di Monterzuolo, a representative from the new government who has been sent to persuade the Prince to join its ranks. Their conversation represents Lampedusa's most pessimistic view of his fellow Sicilians. As Chevalley flatters the aristocrat, Salina responds with a distinct lack of enthusiasm seemingly born from centuries of inertia. He claims that the Sicilian soul has seen great civilisations come and go whilst the island remains a colony, thus leading to a form of utter exhaustion — an exhaustion reflected in the Prince's subsequent death in Palermo's Hotel Trinacria.

The book does not end with its chief protagonist's demise, but continues to tell its readers the fate of the remaining characters, namely Concetta, Carolina and Caterina, Prince Salina's daughters. All three have inherited the religious gene so present in both the fictional Salina family and Lampedusa's own ancestry. They meet with Angelica who recounts the forty years she spent living with Tancredi, whose noble ways had evidently left a mark on his wife's behaviour and interests. The reminiscences of the aged women and their guest, Senator Tassoni, bring a melancholic close to the story as the dynasty fades into bitter-sweet memory.

One of those who voted for the book to receive the Strega Prize was the aristocrat and film director Luchino Visconti (1906–76). According to screenwriter Suso Cecchi d'Amico, Visconti had voted for Lampedusa rather than for his friend Pasolini. In 1960, the director attended a preview of a television documentary entitled *La Sicilia del Gattopardo*, shot on location in Sicily, and the seed was sown to make a film version of the book. In May 1962 the actor Burt Lancaster (1913–94) arrived at The Palms days before he was due to start filming the part of Prince Salina. Lancaster had been chosen to play the leading role despite the fact that he did not speak Italian, however the American had been taking matters in earnest, travelling with a copy of the book and even beginning to learn the language.

On the surface, Lancaster's arrival would appear to be the spark that ignited the keenly anticipated project. In fact, the filming had already started with the shooting of battle sequences designed to portray Garibaldi's Redshirts in the streets of Palermo. As is the case on so many film sets, the monumental moments on screen had their subtle undertow off screen. Alberto Anile and M. Gabriella Giannice detail the machinations behind the scenes in their book, *Operazione Gattopardo*. Visconti had in fact told Lancaster to remain in Rome until he was needed, thus allowing the director to concentrate on the street scenes.

Visconti was determined to use authentic locations *in situ*. For the battle, he set up his film crew in front of the Palazzo Sclafani by Piazza San Giovanni Decollato near to the archway over Via Biscottari. Bystanders were cordoned off from the action by the local police and the streets were strewn with the dust that would have covered nineteenth-century Palermo. The director went out of his way to inform journalists that the Palermitani had been very welcoming — something that could not be said of the local government in the town of Palma di Montechiaro on the south coast. Despite being a key Lampedusan location, the *commune* sent the producer and director a telegram distinctly lacking in hospitality. There were rumblings of mafia discontent.

Visconti's decision to delay Lancaster's arrival at The Palms may have had more than just logistics at its core. From the very beginning he had been searching in a very different direction for his leading man. He had initially looked towards Russian cinema, specifically the actor Nikolay Cherkasov, who had been one of Sergei Eisenstein's favourites. However a recent photo sent from the Russian Embassy persuaded Visconti to drop the idea, given Cherkasov's advancing years and slight appearance. Italian names such as Turi Ferro and Marcello Mastroianni were also considered as was Lawrence Olivier. Anile and Giannice even suggest that Olivier was actually offered the part but refused either due to health or family reasons.

The push for an American star came from the producer Goffredo Lombardo who was aware that the casting would bring in much-needed funding. Visconti's reaction to the suggestion of Lancaster was one of horror, believing that the actor was merely a cowboy. Names such as Marlon Brandon or Anthony Quinn were hastily suggested as alternatives who acted outside the strict confines of genre cinema, but Lombardo was fixed on his original choice. It was the 1961 film *Judgment at Nuremberg* that finally persuaded Visconti of Lancaster's quality as a serious actor, capable of lending subtlety to the role of Prince Salina. Even so, Visconti was unaware of the manoeuvres of those behind the funding who went on a mission to woo the American actor. Although Visconti accepted Lancaster, he never forgot the way in which he had been manipulated to make the choice.

Whilst Lancaster was kicking his heels in Rome, he was not immune to the attentions of the *paparazzi*. The influx of American and English actors in the city had led to even more opportunistic photographers haunting the hot spots, especially Via Veneto where the stars would relax, drink and party. One night in 1958 the English actor Anthony Steel emerged from a nightclub with his wife, Anita Ekberg. Shawn Levy in *Dolce Vita Confidential* tells us that the couple were being watched by one of the leading photographers of the day, Tazio Secchiaroli, who managed to fire off a couple of quick snaps before Steel's explosive and drunken temper swung into action. Waving his arms wildly and intent on attacking Secchiaroli, Steel missed his step, staggered and gave up the pursuit — too worse for wear to cause any serious damage.

When Burt Lancaster was snapped by Umberto Spagna emerging from a restaurant in Piazza Navona with the young actress, Béatrice Altariba, the *paparazzo* was not as fortunate as Secchiaroli. The sturdily-built Lancaster kicked Spagna in the lower abdomen with such force that the photographer was hospitalised for a short while. Without today's twenty-four-hour social media, the pair were able to reach a supposedly amicable agreement that hushed up the incident. It was a somewhat tetchy actor who arrived in Palermo, already suspecting that Visconti would gain the upper hand during filming and that the interpretation of Prince Salina would be the director's and not his.

One of the most unlikely meetings during Lancaster's stay in Sicily was between the actor and that permanent resident of The Palms, Baron Di Stefano. Philippe Fusaro in *Palermo solo* imagines the actor sharing Di Stefano's choice of fish at the aristocrat's habitual table whilst they are joined by a Frenchman whose name the Baron is unable to recall, presumably Alain Delon who played Tancredi. Fusaro visualises an impressed Di Stefano recalling the fine and intelligent words of Signor Lancaster.

This seemingly far-fetched evocation is based on fact. Giuseppe Di Stefano did eat with Burt Lancaster, although we have not been able to establish whether they were joined by Delon or, indeed, any other members of the cast. However, there is one element in the description of the meal as it appears in *Palermo solo* that teeters on the brink of impossibility, namely that Di Stefano was impressed with the refined and sage words of the American actor. This completely ignores the fact that the Baron had Sicilian as his first language and Italian as his second, which was frequently punctuated with Sicilianisms. There is no evidence that he spoke English. We already know that Lancaster was a beginner in Italian and, therefore, the conversation would not have been able to reach the heights of intellectual thought, let alone move beyond polite introduction, unless an interpreter had been present.

Much to the annoyance of Visconti, Lancaster had insisted that his scenes on set be directed and shot in English. The two final versions of the film have Lancaster's voice in English rendition for the release that was otherwise dubbed from Italian for the American audience, and his voice dubbed into Italian by Corrado Gaipa for the rest of the world. The continuing tensions on set led to the establishment of opposing factions, with Delon and the majority of the Italian cast in Visconti's camp and Lancaster with his small American contingent in the other; this included his personal make-up artist who was the only person he would allow to act as his stylist on set.

The scene that pushed everyone to the limit was the memorable ballroom sequence that took place in Palermo's Palazzo Gangi, just to the east of Via Roma. Over thirty-six consecutive nights, the crew grappled with the complications of filming. The number of costumes required spiralled into the hundreds, furniture was loaned by Lampedusa's adopted son Gioacchino Lanza Tomasi, and extras milled about in all directions. Visconti had chosen the searing heat of August for this enterprise with unsurprising consequences, especially as the temperatures remained at a torrid thirty-five degrees even during the night-time filming. Anile and Giannice claim that a Red Cross van was permanently parked outside the Gangi for the duration, attending to cast members who had fainted as well as those suffering from other heat-related complaints.

Visconti also found the lighting situation difficult, particularly due to the many candles, candelabras and chandeliers required for realism. It appears that eliminating studio lights from the field of view became a problem, adding to the issues of heat and the need for re-shooting. Things came to a head when Lancaster, suffering from a swollen knee, had to perform a dance scene with Claudia Cardinale who was playing the part of Tancredi's fiancée. Cardinale recalls Visconti shouting at Lancaster to stop whining and suffer in silence, blaming the actor for insisting that he go for an early morning run each day to perpetuate the illusion that he was still young. In *Operazione Gattopardo*, the authors go further with Visconti's insult and quote the production manager, Pietro Notarianni, as remembering the director, in front of all the cast, alluding to the fact that Lancaster was no Mittel-European prince but a mere cowboy.

Apparently, Lancaster drew himself up to his full height and slowly approached the director who told Notarianni to remain by his side, despite the fact that he wished to leave them to their argument. A torrent of English abuse came from the star's lips whilst Visconti simply sat without saying a word. The final slur at the end of this litany was that Visconti lacked the appropriate manners. This accusation hit home and the director had to admit that he had overstepped the mark on this occasion. The irritability amongst the two camps brought on by heat and differences of opinion was bound to erupt into a full-blown argument of this nature. Tensions, having been released, created a *rapprochement* between Lancaster and Visconti culminating in a respectful concern for each other's opinions and an enduring friendship.

With the arrival of his family, Lancaster decided to move away from The Palms and hire a residence known as the Villa Scalea ai Colli on the way to Mondello. His wife and five children moved in with him and they also hired a yacht for excursions between Mondello, Addaura and Palermo. In this sense he was emulating Visconti who had a dislike of hotels and had already installed himself in a converted castle along with a coterie of friends and his personal staff. In casting around for a model on which to base his interpretation of Prince Salina, Lancaster needed to look no further than the director himself.

Visconti represented many of the contradictions present in Italian society at the time. Formally, he was known as the Count of Lonate Pozzolo, a settlement in the province of Varese to the north of the region of Lombardy. He was born in Milan, one of seven children whose father bore the rather grandiose title of Giuseppe Visconti di Modrone, Duke of Grazzano Visconti and Count of Lonate Pozzolo. The young Luchino's privileged upbringing allowed him to study the cello and mix with the highest achievers in the worlds of art and theatre.

His film career started in 1935 when he worked as an assistant director on Jean Renoir's *Toni*. It was the 1948 film *La terra trema* (*The Earth Trembles*) that launched him as an innovative director in his own right. The film, using only amateur actors from the vicinity of Aci Trezza on Sicily's east coast, is loosely based on Giovanni Verga's classic novel *I Malavoglia* (*The House by the Medlar Tree*). It tells of the exploitation of a working-class fishing family who mortgaged their house in order to try and circumvent the low prices of wholesalers who controlled the market. When the family boat is lost at sea, their fortunes go from bad to worse. We can see from the subject matter that despite his wealthy background Visconti had a social conscience.

During World War II Visconti joined the Italian Communist Party. Although he may not have been a full-blown Marxist by conviction, he was certainly a fellow traveller. It is in this context that critics were expecting his version of *The Leopard* to be a left-wing response to what was generally perceived as a novel written from a right-wing perspective. The Spanish commentator and writer Luis Antonio de Villena believes that the film has the virtue of reflecting both the contemporary situation and the past in which it was set, thereby capturing the timeless quality of high art.

For many in the 1960s, *The Leopard* was a film that represented the inescapable decay of history's ruling classes, the morally bankrupt aristocracy of yesteryear; a message that could also be applied to the increasingly corrupt Christian Democrat politicians of the day who were ripe for a challenge from the proletariat and students with vivid new ideas — witness the events of 1968. Significantly, Visconti chose to remove the death of Prince Salina and the subsequent chapter detailing the fate of his three daughters. Although the ending of the text has a melancholic poignancy, particularly with regard to Concetta's realisation that Tancredi had always loved her, it also prolongs the story beyond the life of the Prince and provides the glimpse of a possible alternative history.

The left-wing critic Antonello Trombadori felt that the removal of Prince Salina's death and the subsequent chapter were significant in refocusing the film, thereby rendering it both faithful to the book yet enabling it to be a barbed comment on the state of political transformation. De Villena, in *El Gatopardo: La transformación y el abismo* (*The Leopard: Transformation and the Abyss*), is sure that Lampedusa thought the old ruling class would be a better prospect than the bourgeoisie and petit-bourgeoisie that was bound to replace it, even though it was significantly flawed.

The nature of change is at the heart of both the book and the film. Does Sicily want to be the kind of society where change is superficial, where aristocrats can duel in the foyer of The Palms and suffer few consequences? Or does it want change to come at the deepest level, where the rules apply to everyone, irrespective of notable position or underworld connection? If Lampedusa's vision was worn down by Salina's centuries of exhaustion, then Visconti's supposed view of the Marxist march towards the end of history could be seen as equally challenging but also defective. Modern Sicily has had to adapt, not only to a rapidly changing geo-political world, but also to internal circumstances only partially understood, if not wholly predicted, by both author and director.

That is not to say that Lampedusa's vision was one of simple despondent disillusion, disappointment solved only by death. In his words you can occasionally read a *cri de coeur* — a call to slough the dust of centuries which has become a second skin for some Sicilians of Prince Salina's breed. The island's inaction is reflected in the author's own life. Apart from his service in World War I, much of Lampedusa's time was spent as a reclusive dilettante, dabbling at the edges of both thought and life. It was only when he found his literary voice that all those years of close observation came tumbling forth in a mixture of cynicism and frustration.

Irrespective of political viewpoint, the novel and the film manage to convey an island rich in sensory experience. The language of the novel is brimming with beautifully crafted imagery that enables us to feel the heat of an intense summer or imagine the robust, concentrated flavours of Prince Salina's table. Likewise, one of Visconti's most memorable and evocative scenes concerns the family's arrival at their country seat of Donnafugata after a long hot journey by carriage. The Salinas, along with Tancredi, repair to the Chiesa Madre to hear a *Te Deum*. The camera pans along the carved choir stalls where the family are seated, still wearing their travelling attire which is noticeably covered in a film of fine sand and dirt. The message is at once both subtle and blatant — they are consigned to the past, no longer useful or relevant but preserved in a *tableau* as a *memento mori*. The warning again focuses on change and the dangers of stasis, a paralysis that could lead the family to a form of mummification, reminiscent of the embalmed corpses in Palermo's Capuchin Catacombs, caught forever in their dusty finery.

One aspect of modern Sicily's obsession with *The Leopard* that would have surprised Visconti and Lampedusa is the commercialisation which surrounds the film and book. To the twenty-first-century reader, this is perhaps less surprising, as any successful entity inevitably develops a commercial persona. There are tours in the footsteps of Lampedusa's Prince Salina and a Parco Letterario del Gattopardo (a literary foundation) is located in the reconstructed ruins of the real Donnafugata at Santa Margherita di Belìce. There is also the Parco Culturale del Gattopardo — Giuseppe Tomasi di Lampedusa, run by Sicilia Letteraria in Palermo, where tourists can relive scenes from the film and discover all the locations associated with the author of the book. We realise, of course, that with this text and our previous work on literary Sicily, we are but one more contributor to a story passing into legend.

The barman of The Palms, Toti Librizzi, is the man who recalled Burt Lancaster's meeting with Baron Di Stefano and he is also the person responsible for creating the now-famous Gattopardo cocktail which could once be ordered in the hotel's bar of the same name. Sadly, it will no longer be mixed by Toti who has retired to his country house. The eponymous drink, a heady brew, consists of one part Hennessy cognac, two parts Grand Marnier, four parts fresh orange juice and three parts strawberry juice. The mixture is tipped into an ice-filled glass, topped with an orange segment and completed with a squeeze of lemon juice. Clearly, Lampedusa would never have tried the cocktail as it was invented after his death, but we suspect it may not have been to his taste. Librizzi though recalls staff mentioning that Lampedusa would occasionally stop by for a drink at the bar which, unbeknownst to him, would in future bear the name of his most famous character.

It is thanks to Toti Librizzi that the wider public know of the celebrated imbibers who took a drink or two at the hotel's bar. In Mirto, near Capo d'Orlando on Sicily's north coast, Toti has created the Casa museo della memoria, a small museum containing his collection of memorabilia from his time at The Palms. The museum is managed by the cultural association La Casa di Colapesce — named after the mythical Sicilian boy diver who prevents the island from sinking by holding it up from under the sea. Librizzi kept a book that he would ask his illustrious customers to illustrate and sign, and these autographs and doodles form a significant part of his display, together with photographs and other keepsakes from his years as a barman, including objects that once belonged to the famous clientele of the hotel.

The respected Sicilian writer Vincenzo Consolo was present at the association's inauguration and his warm words are immortalised on its website. Consolo, in admiration of Librizzi's wisdom and intelligence, calls his autograph collection a 'golden book' composed of marks made by a diverse range of characters who have set foot in the hotel and whose paths may or may not have crossed on the way to order a drink at the bar. He refers to the hotel as a 'Calvinian castle' — a direct reference to Italo Calvino's work *The Castle of Crossed Destinies* (*Il castello dei destini incrociati*), a novel that tells its story of fateful coincidence and predestination through the reading of tarot cards.

By listing some of the hotel's most famous guests, Consolo conjures the establishment's historic quality and laments the inability of the walls to speak. From painters, musicians, writers and poets to actors, singers, dancers, directors, scientists and politicians, all have left their designs in Librizzi's golden book. Leafing through the entries, Consolo feels that any reader would want to 'ask questions, form hypotheses and speculate: what motivated these characters to come to Palermo; which of them had the occasion to meet and what events arose from those meetings?' He goes on to suggest that 'a novel could then be written; the fascinating story of Palermo's Palms Hotel'. Consolo, who died in 2012, was sadly never to write such a book, but the journalist Melinda Zacco has attempted just such a project with her novel *Il mondo in un cassetto al Grand Hotel delle Palme* (*The Grand Hotel delle Palme: The World in a Drawer*). Whatever the merits of the text, Zacco is without Consolo's considerable reputation and therefore the work has gone largely unnoticed.

No speculation is required in order to understand why the opera diva Maria Callas (1923–77) visited Palermo and stayed at The Palms. The Teatro Massimo was, by the 1950s, firmly fixed on the itinerary of touring performers. In 1951, Callas was about to perform Bellini's opera, *Norma*, at the Massimo in Palermo on the one hundred and fiftieth anniversary of the composer's birth. Before having the chance to unpack, she received an urgent call from Antonio Ghiringhelli, the manager of La Scala. He wanted her to drop everything and rush back to Milan so she could take over the role of Aida in the opera of the same name in place of the indisposed Renata Tebaldi. The insulted Callas had already deputised in the previous year and refused point blank in the hope that Ghiringhelli would eventually turn to her as the first choice for a lead role. Staying in Palermo to honour her contract was a wise decision as those who saw her performance remember it to this day.

Doubtless, it was her acclaim that prompted Baron Di Stefano to invite Callas to dine with him. It was far from the last time that the diva would sing at the Teatro Massimo or visit The Palms. Festivities shared with Di Stefano did not help the singer's battle with her portly figure. During the 1950s, Callas realised that the increasing pounds were affecting her voice and health in general. She is reported as saying that movement on stage was becoming difficult, causing tiredness and excessive perspiration. By the mid-1950s she had managed to lose an astonishing amount of weight, an achievement that led reporters and the paparazzi to hound the now svelte Greek diva. Scurrilous reports attributed her dramatic change in figure to anything from a particular type of pasta to a tapeworm. The real secret was nothing more than a sensible diet of healthy food.

It is true to say, however, that scandal often dogged Callas' career. After filing a lawsuit against the pasta company that had taken the credit for her weight loss, she was on the receiving end of another lawsuit filed in 1955 by a certain Eddy Bagarozy who claimed to be her agent. The same year, *Time* magazine ran a controversial cover story which portrayed the singer's relationship with her mother as problematic, hinting that this was behind her temperamental behaviour. Maria never really forgave her mother for condemning her looks and forcing her to give up a normal childhood in order to sing and make money for the family.

Just as Callas was establishing her opera career, a more self-effacing personality was also reaching the heights in her chosen field, ballet. Carla Fracci (b. 1936) was another celebrity to dine at the table of the hotel's now permanently resident aristocrat. Fracci was born in Milan and studied dance at La Scala's school of ballet. From 1958 onwards, she performed as a prima ballerina and danced in various companies worldwide, partnering the likes of Rudolf Nureyev, Mikhail Baryshnikov and Erik Bruhn with whom she filmed a version of Adolphe Adam's *Giselle* in 1969. The poet Eugenio Montale dedicated a poem to Fracci called 'La danzatrice stanca' ('The Tired Dancer'), which he wrote during her pregnancy in 1969, lamenting her absence from the stage and comparing a ballet without her to a 'deathly pageant'.

Another frequenter of The Palms was an actor who made a career from the dark demands of death, namely Christopher Lee (1922–2015), the quintessential portrayer of the aristocratic vampire, Dracula. Lee made an entry in Librizzi's volume and would have had much to chat about with the genial barman. The subjects covered must have veered away from the fictitious realms of the undead to the far more serious topic of war, given Lee's military connection with the island. Behind the actor's urbane mask lay a fascinating backstory that included a significant Sicilian element. Lee, whose full name was Christopher Frank Carandini Lee, was born to an English father and a mother with a noteworthy Italian lineage. Countess Estelle Marie Carandini di Sarzano could trace her ancestors all the way back to Charlemagne via Italian political refugees and opera singers.

Before he could be conscripted without a choice of service, Lee made the decision in 1941 to join the British Royal Air Force. However, whilst training in Southern Africa he experienced headaches which were a result of a failed optic nerve, putting an end to his flying career before it had even started. Extremely disappointed, he searched for an alternative meaningful role and applied to join RAF Intelligence. By May 1943 he was in the city of Zuwarah, Libya, awaiting the invasion of Sicily. Lee was to see action on the beaches of Pachino, in the island's south-east corner, where the majority of British troops landed. As the forces made their way along Sicily's Ionian coast, the future actor and his squadron made a permanent base at Agnone Bagni.

A recurring bout of malaria took Lee away from his unit and he was flown back to Carthage for treatment in a field hospital. On his return to the squadron, he found his men on the brink of mutiny, frustrated by a lack of mail and alcohol but, most importantly, information. Like any intelligence officer worth his salt, Lee had kept up to speed with the conflict's most significant developments, especially those on the eastern front. In later interviews, he recalled the moment when he bombarded those under his command with a relentless stream of facts and figures to the extent that he was sure they must have regretted asking him in the first place.

In another interview with the Irish television presenter Terry Wogan, Lee was asked directly if he had been a spy during the war. Drawing himself up to his full height of over six foot five inches, he threw the question back at Wogan by suggesting that he would not have exactly blended into the background, although his knowledge of French and Italian would undoubtedly have been an asset. Lee was happy to talk about the generalities of his war experience but, like so many veterans, he rarely discussed the minutiae of the horrors he had witnessed. The invasion of Italy was, at times, a brutal campaign and Lee witnessed much suffering that stayed with him forever.

A small glimpse into the experiences he had compartmentalised, out of necessity, can be seen from an incident on the set of the *Lord of the Rings*. Lee was playing the role of the wizard, Saruman, who was to be stabbed in the back by Grima Wormtongue. The director, Peter Jackson, asked Lee to let out a scream as the knife plunged between his shoulder blades. Calmly, the aging actor turned to Jackson and informed him that he had witnessed men being stabbed in such a manner and that none of them had ever screamed; they had merely issued a biological sigh as the air left their lungs. The scene never appeared in the version released for the cinema but can be found in the extended trilogy on DVD.

Lee might never have become an actor if it had not been for a post-war encounter with one of his Italian relatives. Nicolò Carandini, his cousin and a former minister in Bonomi's anti-Fascist government, had been appointed as Italian Ambassador to Britain. During a lunchtime chat, Lee was weighing up his future career options and describing his wartime experiences when Carandini made the suggestion that his cousin take up acting. Lee was enthused by the idea and was put in touch with Nicolò's friend, the film producer, Filippo Del Giudice. It would be another ten years, however, before stardom arrived.

Despite a breadth of acting experience, the charming Lee is inevitably best-known for his Hammer Horror movies that spanned the period from 1957 to 1976. It is little remembered that the actor also appeared in Italian films such as the 1961 movie *Ercole al centro della terra*, known in English as *Hercules in the Haunted World* and *Il castello dei morti vivi* (*The Castle of the Living Dead*) in 1964. By the 1970s, the sugar-coated façade of Italy's *dolce vita* had soured but its love affair with cinema and the arts had survived intact. The years of post-war introspection and rapid boom had produced much more than starlets, grandiose parties, truculent actors, throw-away films and chancers with a camera.

In 1975 Toti Librizzi was made head barman at The Palms and the artist Renato Guttuso (1912–87) asked him for his by now celebrated book so that he could add a congratulatory carnation in vivid colours. Guttuso was a man of the left but was, nevertheless, happy to share a drink with Baron Di Stefano. He had shown his political leanings as early as the Spanish Civil War, during which time he contributed to the magazine *Corrente di Vita*. Guttuso painted *Fucilazione in Campagna* (*A Shooting in the Countryside*), a work he dedicated to Federico García Lorca, the Spanish poet who had been executed by Francoist troops.

Some of Guttuso's work concerned Sicily's struggle for land reform, an ongoing battle almost as eternal as the Sicilian landscape. He also painted the *zolfatari*, the workers who suffered intolerable conditions in the island's sulphur mines (see chapter 1), conditions described previously by Luigi Pirandello and Guy de Maupassant amongst others. Guttuso was a native of Bagheria, the former playground for Palermo's aristocrats and, as we know, now a warren of ill-constructed streets that seemingly lead nowhere, but which will occasionally launch the unsuspecting visitor towards the gates of a noble villa. Like many before him, he was drawn to the Villa Palagonia and its monstrous guardians. He produced more than one painting of the edifice with the most famous of these portraying a barrier of prickly pears in the foreground, masking the surrounding garden wall from which the contorted gargoyles leer mockingly.

A collection of Guttoso's works are now housed in Bagheria's Villa Cattolica where his ashes are also kept in a tomb that can be seen in the grounds of the villa. However, to view his most celebrated work, *La Vucciria*, the visitor will need to seek out the Palazzo Chiaramonte-Steri in Piazza Marina, the former Inquisition prison, where the painting is now displayed in a room to the right of the antiquated cells that still bear the heartbreaking graffiti of the Holy Office's desperate prisoners.

The vibrant canvas conveys all the energy once found during the heyday of Palermo's Vucciria market. The eye is drawn to the central figure of a retreating woman in a body-skimming white dress sashaying her way between the stalls; some believe her to be Guttuso's mistress. She faces a representation of the painter in a yellow jumper, who is perhaps accompanied by his wife. On the left, a decapitated swordfish, mouth gaping and eyes angry, sits amid its sliced body, surrounded by a less impressive catch. A bank of fresh fruit and vegetables in primary colours twists the perspective of the image to the right, leading the eye to a table of cheeses that gives way to the sudden intrusion of a suspended, bisected carcass. The sensual, earthy composition has an undertow of threat represented by the butcher who, knife in hand, carves steaks from the carcass.

Guttuso's style initially developed in response to Fascism and was dubbed 'social art', moving away from abstraction and also naturalism. His palette reflected the strong colours of his native island with vivid blues, sulphurous yellows and reptilian greens. In 1971 Guttuso was awarded an honorary degree from the University of Palermo, the same year in which a major retrospective of his work was held in the Palazzo dei Normanni. The exhibition catalogue was introduced by his friend, Leonardo Sciascia, who was writing his text on the death of Raymond Roussel during the same period. Sciascia would occasionally join Guttuso in the Gattopardo bar and no doubt they discussed their shared world view.

Another artist who made some sketches for Toti Librizzi was Giorgio de Chirico (1888–1978), born to a Genoese-Greek mother and a Sicilian father in the Greek town of Volos. In his autobiography, *Memorie della mia vita (Memories of My Life)*, he recalls being tutored by a drawing instructor called Barbieri who had come to Greece to look for work but had found the economic situation just as problematic as in Italy. It was only de Chirico's passion for art that enabled him to bear the stench of stale retsina and garlic emanating from his expatriate teacher.

De Chirico, in his early years, developed a style that would become known as metaphysical art — a term used to describe the dreamlike qualities of his canvases which often carried a sinister undercurrent. The painter's surrealist work *The Song of Love* precedes André Breton's movement, formed in 1924, by ten years. The composition is made up of a Greek bust set against a plastered façade, to which is pinned a huge red surgeon's glove. On the floor in the foreground sits a green ball and a steam train is disappearing on the horizon. These disparate and seemingly unconnected objects reflect the subconscious dream state with the glove lending an ominous presence.

By the 1960s, de Chirico was influencing filmmakers such as Michelangelo Antonioni, while the 1976 film *Il deserto dei Tartari* (*The Desert of the Tartars*) by the director Valerio Zurlini has undeniable stylistic links to the imagery of the artist. The film, based on a story by Dino Buzzati — also the author of *La famosa invasione degli orsi in Sicilia* (*The Bears' Famous Invasion of Sicily*) — follows a young officer, Giovanni Drogo, as he guards the Bastiani fortress from an imminent attack by the Tartars. The role of Colonel Giovanbattista Filimore is played by Vittorio Gassman (1922–2000), another star in Librizzi's collection.

Gassman, as his name suggests, had a German father, but he is inextricably linked with the rise of Italian cinema. The actor is remembered fondly for his talent and professionalism which made him one of Italy's leading performers. He starred in everything from twentieth-century classics like *A Streetcar Named Desire* to Shakespeare and the plays of Aeschylus. Luchino Visconti was a big influence in developing his career, which inevitably came to the notice of Hollywood. Gassman's second wife was the American actress, Shelley Winters, and their subsequent split due to the actor's affair with his young co-star, Anna Maria Ferrero, provided many tabloid column inches, especially when Gassman and Winters were contractually obliged to appear together on the set of *Mambo* in Rome.

Such was Winters' fury over the affair, she tried to attack her younger rival in a fit of anger and it was left to Gassman to step between the pair of warring women before any damage could be done. We have read an account which says this incident took place at the Teatro Carlo Felice in Genoa and another that places the attack on the *Mambo* film set. The episode was immortalised by Walter Molino who designed the illustrations for the magazine *La Domenica del Corriere*. The comic-strip style print, tinged with a degree of photorealism, shows a stumbling Ferrero backing away from an irate Shelly Winters whose raised hand is being restrained by a dismayed Gassman; her other hand is clenched in a threatening fist. In the background, concerned onlookers throw disapproving glances over their shoulders.

This public display must have been intensely embarrassing for Gassman who was otherwise a cultured individual. He turned to theatre and books for solace, citing Herman Melville's acclaimed *Moby Dick* as a favourite. In an interview with the newspaper *Corriere della Sera*, Gassman described Melville as a giant and stated that his magnum opus had been a companion throughout his career. He called it a 'symbolic book, a secular Bible'. He admitted to the interviewer that he knew large segments of the text almost by heart. It was a recital of *Moby Dick* that brought Gassman to The Palms where he doodled a ship caught in a storm for Toti the barman. It was not his only visit.

Gassman could play in Hollywood movies with ease owing to his fluency in English. Anglophone actors keen to play roles in Italian cinema, with the notable exception of Christopher Lee, had to face the perils of dubbing. It is a credit to Burt Lancaster that his performance overrides the obvious voice substitution found on the soundtrack of the Italian release. Lancaster also paved the way for Richard Burton (1925–84) who accepted the part of Cesare Braggi in Vittorio de Sica's final film, *Il Viaggio* (*The Voyage*, sometimes known as *The Journey*). He played opposite fellow Briton Ian Bannen and the Italian siren, Sophia Loren.

Certain scenes from the movie were shot on location in Sicily, specifically in Syracuse, the Baroque town of Noto and Palermo, hence Burton and Loren's stay at The Palms. De Sica already had an illustrious career behind him and two years prior to the release of *Il Viaggio* in 1970 he had received the Academy Award for Best Foreign Language Film for *Il giardino dei Finzi-Contini* (*The Garden of the Finzi-Continis*), based on Giorgio Bassani's masterpiece of the same name. For the Burton and Loren project he had decided to adapt a story written by the Sicilian Nobel Laureate, Luigi Pirandello. He took the text from the author's collection of short stories, *Novelle per un anno* (*Short Stories for a Year*).

Set just before the outbreak of World War I, Count Cesare Braggi has to forgo his love for the seamstress Adriana De Mauro (Sophia Loren) who, according to the dying wish of Cesare's father, is destined to marry his brother, Antonio, played by Bannen. The unfortunate Antonio dies in a car accident leaving Adriana to bring up their son whilst descending into a long period of mourning. It is Cesare who manages to revive the widow's lust for life only to discover that she is dying from an incurable disease. The diagnosis of a Palermo cardiologist is confirmed by a similar specialist in Naples. With little time left, the hitherto repressed love between Cesare and Adriana flourishes, leading to the final scenes in Venice where Loren's character dies.

Richard Burton had his own demons to fight whilst portraying Braggi's tragic destiny. According to Sophia Loren's memoir, *Yesterday, Today, Tomorrow: My Life*, the Welsh star was battling with his alcohol addiction and struggling to hold together his fated romance with Elizabeth Taylor (1932–2011). Prior to shooting, Burton contacted Loren with the unusual request that he might be allowed to stay with her and her husband in Rome in order to avoid the attentions of the paparazzi. He needed a quiet, domestic environment in which to 'get back in shape', by which he meant to temper the self-destructive boozing that had been such a feature of his life in preceding years.

On one disastrous evening in 1968, Burton had been drinking heavily with his brother, Ifor, who had come to visit him in Switzerland. Ifor lost his balance and fell so awkwardly that he broke his neck and was severely paralysed. According to their younger brother Graham, this may have been a significant contributory factor in Burton's almost suicidal levels of alcohol abuse, particularly after Ifor's death in 1972. Despite the fact that Loren claimed the Welshman was an exemplary house guest, de Sica, whilst observing the actor on set, felt that Burton was on a path to an early grave. His concerned observations also saw the effect that the tempestuous 'Elizabetta' was having on his demeanour.

Elizabetta is, of course, Elizabeth Taylor who, prior to the first camera roll, had phoned Burton and demanded he be by her side in Los Angeles where she was to have an operation. The resigned but dutiful actor made the thirty-hour round trip which allowed him just a short time to be at her bedside before making it back in time for the first scenes. At this point in their relationship, the couple were heading inexorably for divorce, notwithstanding a short period of reconciliation that saw them spend the Christmas of 1973 together in Puerta Vallarta, Mexico.

Both were prone to affairs, particularly during rocky times in their marriage and long periods of separation. During the filming of *Il Viaggio*, Taylor started an affair with a businessman, Henry Wynberg, who had the unlikely profession of used-car salesman. Melvyn Bragg in his biography *Rich: The Life of Richard Burton*, says that Elizabeth was convinced that her husband was having an affair with Sophia Loren.

The most Loren ever admitted to, in an interview with *The Telegraph*, was her admiration for his looks, voice and acting skills. The photographer Gianni Bozzacchi, who worked closely with Taylor, has claimed in his memoir that everyone on set and in the press was convinced of an affair between the two co-stars. He does admit, however, that he had no way of knowing the exact truth. The rumours cannot be substantiated.

Sicily was close to the hearts of both Burton and Taylor. It was to the island that the couple escaped in 1963 when they first became an item during the filming of *Cleopatra* in Rome. The A-list magnet resort of Taormina on the Ionian coast was their destination, where the San Domenico Palace Hotel, once a monastery, has even preserved the wrought-iron bed that witnessed their passionate encounters. Taormina was also the scene of their petty and not-so-petty jealousies with reports of Taylor becoming so possessed by the green-eyed monster that she felt compelled to smash a guitar over Burton's head.

The reception of *Il Viaggio* was nowhere near as dramatic as its filming. The *New York Times* felt that de Sica had succumbed to a bout of sentimentality which was out of sync with the world around him. Its view on the casting of Burton and Bannen mentions the oddity of their dubbing in Italian, although their original voices are used in the English version. It is not this, however, that incurs the newspaper's strongest criticism, which concerns the miscasting of all the major roles due to a mismatch in age and the inability of the Britons to feel at home in the Sicilian landscape. The film is sumptuous in its period detail and locational cinematography, but we have to agree that the final product is something of a damp squib, even though Sophia Loren received the prestigious Italian David di Donatello award for best actress.

The music for the film was composed by Manuel de Sica, Vittorio's son with the actress María Mercader, who, bizarrely, was the half-sister of Leon Trotsky's assassin. Manuel de Sica spent time on the set and with the actors in The Palms, gaining inspiration for the soundtrack. The piece accompanying the film title is a gently lilting, melancholic tune led by the simple notes of a piano, backed by strings that faintly echo Pietro Mascagni's *Intermezzo* from *Cavalleria Rusticana*.

The gentle music of the film score was a world away from the *trova* guitar of Máximo Francisco Repilado Muñoz Telles (1907–2003), otherwise known as Compay Segundo. The Cuban guitarist arrived in Palermo a year after de Sica and his crew had left, having been asked by the Palermo City Council to perform a concert at the Villa Trabia in Via Antonino Salinas, a twenty-minute walk from The Palms. In the romantic surroundings of this eighteenth-century classical villa, set in a park with a bridge and ornate fountain, Compay and his musicians performed from his repertoire of *sones*, *danzones* and mambo beats — blending African and Spanish rhythms. The troupe was staying at The Palms and Toti Librizzi recalls Compay heading for the restaurant after their set at the villa. He paused in front of the Gattopardo bar and doffed his Panama hat as if recognising the gentility of a bygone era.

Librizzi was much taken with the gesture and invited the guitarist to have a drink with him after he had finished his meal. The pair struck up an unlikely friendship and Compay headed for the bar as his first port of call when he came back to Palermo during the heady years of the famous *Buena Vista Social Club*, the 1996 album promoted and directed by the North-American musician Ry Cooder and subsequently filmed by Wim Wenders. With his illustrious compatriots, Compay played some of his famous tunes at the Teatro di Verdura, compositions which included 'Chan Chan', the track with which he will forever be associated. The guitarist's hat, which Compay had given to Toti, is now on display in the barman's Casa museo della memoria.

The robust Compay had boasted to Librizzi that he would live to be a magnificent one hundred and sixteen, seemingly plenty of time for the Sicilian to visit him in Cuba, however he died in 2003, at the age of ninety-five, before the barman had the chance to visit the musician's home. Librizzi was then instrumental in setting up a cultural exhibit at Havana's Museo Maqueta called 'Dai Caraibi al Mediterraneo — Cuba Sicilia'. During the inauguration of the photographic display, Toti slipped away from the celebrations and headed for Santiago de Cuba where Compay is buried in the Santa Ifigenia cemetery. Wearing the stylish Panama hat, he laid flowers at his friend's grave.

Another musician of note to stay at The Palms was Ray Charles (1930–2004), the American soul singer who had been blind from the age of seven. Librizzi was faced with a dilemma when presenting Charles with his golden book, aware that the prospect of contributing something meaningful might make the performer feel uncomfortable. He need not have worried. Charles happily took the pen from the barman, placed his right hand on the page and proceeded to draw around it with his left.

Charles had been used to performing at some of Italy's most renowned historic venues. The Arena di Verona, the Roman amphitheatre usually reserved for opera, had already witnessed the American's performance alongside Italy's foremost blues man, Adelmo Fornaciari, otherwise known as Zucchero. Things were to prove more problematic in Sicily when Charles was scheduled to perform with Renzo Arbore at the historic site of Selinunte, situated on the coast and over an hour's drive to the south of Palermo. The technicians had begun to set up the equipment amongst the Greek temple ruins when they were summarily stopped by the Regional Council for Cultural Heritage.

It was claimed that the archaeological site was not the appropriate cultural location for a concert of this kind. The functionary at the head of the Council felt he could only overturn the ban by using a special dispensation which he was unwilling to do because of the precedent it would set and the problems it would cause. He was backed in this by the President of the Region, head of the regional government. Both feared accusations of an abuse of power, given the opinions expressed by the bodies they represented and those of the local superintendency.

In fact, authorisation for the concert at Selinunte had never been given. The local Municipality of Castelvetrano had buried its head in the sand, hoping for a last-minute change of heart from the superintendency and the aforementioned heritage organisation who had always been in opposition. Desperate attempts by the local mayor fell on deaf ears leading to the final clash between the authorities and Charles' frantic and exasperated technical staff. This incident is indicative of Sicily's dilemma when faced with the need to modernise and attract the tourist dollar but at the same time adhere to a cultural responsibility for the protection of its wealth of antiquities.

Ray Charles and his team were relocated to the far more prosaic Paolo Marino stadium in nearby Castelvetrano where concrete football terraces replaced the ancient ruins set against the inviting Mediterranean. Eight thousand ticket holders squeezed into the confines of the town's football ground, probably many more than would attend a match for a side that now languishes in the distant reaches of Sicily's Regional League, Group A. Twenty-first-century representatives of the local heritage bodies seem to have now come to terms with the use of ancient sites for popular music. Recent concerts at Selinunte have featured the Jamaican hip hop and ragga artist, Sean Paul, in addition to the Dutch house DJ, Martin Garrix. The columns must be vibrating to their millennial foundations.

Charles' soul and Compay Segundo's Cuban rhythms brought the music of the world to Sicilian shores. The sound of Astor Piazzolla (1921–92), the Argentinian bandoneon player, would instantly have felt more familiar, although his music undoubtedly shares common roots with both of the above. It is easy to picture Piazzolla in his room at The Palms, taking his precious bandoneon from its case and running through a handful of the pieces he would be playing later. He was a proponent of *nuevo tango* which incorporated elements of jazz and classical music. Tango itself was born from a mixture of African beats, Spanish tunes and other influences derived from European migration to Argentina and Uruguay, with much of that migration coming from Italy and Sicily.

As his name suggests, Piazzolla was of direct Italian descent. It was Jorge Luis Borges, the respected Argentinian writer, who said in his biography of the poet Evaristo Carriego that the '*criollos viejos*' who gave birth to tango were called 'Bevilacqua, Greco or de Bassi' — all Italian family names. If these were some of the originators, Italians also had much to do with the gentrification of tango, bringing it out of the dark shadows and into the refined salons and middle-class ballrooms. European polkas, tarantellas and mazurkas were added to the mix to produce the music we know today, although the lyrics still maintain an element of immigrant lament. In many ways, they are tunes that Spanish speakers would refer to as *ida y vuelta* songs — composed by those that have gone to the New World and returned home.

Sometime after Piazzolla's death, his wife, the singer Laura Escalada, was in Palermo carrying out her role as manager on tour with the Italian singer, Milva. In conversation with Toti Librizzi at the Gattopardo, the circumstances of her husband's death arose. She recounted his final hours in a clinic following a stroke, suffering from pneumonia and sunk in a coma for days. He died, as he predicted in song, in the early hours of a Buenos Aires morning. The account of Piazzolla's illness reminded

Librizzi of the actress Susan Strasberg and her unfortunate demise from breast cancer. Strasberg had been another of Richard Burton's conquests and they even took an apartment together in New York for a short period. The actress is best known for her role between 1955 and 1957 as Anne Frank in the Broadway production of the famous diary, and for the 1960 Oscar-nominated Italo-Yugoslav film, *Kapò*. A former long-term resident in Italy, she was often referred to as 'La Strasberg'.

It transpired that Escalada had been Susan's friend and made the assertion that the American had actually committed suicide because of her illness. Although the claim cannot be substantiated, the statement hit the barman particularly hard. During his last conversation with Strasberg, she had asked him whether he believed in reincarnation. Not taking the question too seriously, he replied that he thought it likely. When she pursued his reasoning, he quickly and without thinking felt obliged to provide the star with an appropriate answer, specifically he thought it must be the case because he could remember previous lives.

This spurious confession drew Strasberg closer to the barman and from that moment she wanted his attention and time. A photograph exists of Librizzi and Strasberg together standing next to The Palms' Christmas tree, the last Christmas that the actress would see. Five months later, she would be dead. Escalada's revelation and Librizzi's rash championing of reincarnation pricked his sensitive conscience, a regret that stayed with him for many months.

These interconnecting threads that work their way through the fabric of *la dolce vita*, from its glorious inception to its tattered demise, reflect Calvino's crossed destinies, the storied imaginings of the novel that Consolo was never to write. As we have seen, The Palms' role in hosting actors, painters and musicians continued well beyond the intoxicating years of the 1960s, but Hollywood's affair with Italy and Sicily, in particular, had already begun to take a more sinister turn, a twisted fork that would taint the world's view of the island for the foreseeable future.

6

ALTERED IMAGES

If *The Leopard*'s relationship with Sicily is uncomfortable, then *The Godfather*'s, in its literary and cinematic representations, is positively dysfunctional. The story of the rise of Vito Andolini from his Sicilian origins to become Don Corleone has dripped into the collective subconscious, constantly feeding and underlining the island's association with organised crime. Whether listening to a travelogue on Spanish radio, watching a cookery programme on English television or reading a holiday article in the popular American press, it is impossible not to pick up references to the book, published in 1969, and, more often, to Coppola's film trilogy (released between 1972 and 1990). These lazy allusions are trotted out with little thought for the stereotypical implications and their entrenchment.

This is not to detract from the masterly craftsmanship of Francis Ford Coppola's three films, especially the first two, but rather highlights the lasting impact of a successful franchise. Italian directors such as Francesco Rosi had already made films dealing with the complex criminal aspects of Sicilian society, notably *Salvatore Giuliano* (1962), but *The Godfather* migrated the story to America and in so doing contrasted the gap in circumstances between the two places. The American experience, by definition, lent a certain nostalgia to the island and its role in begetting the mafia, a wistfulness that compares unfavourably with the harsh and brutal origins of the modern organisation amongst the enforcers who patrolled the orange groves of Palermo's Conca d'Oro in the nineteenth century.

All three of the films have segments set in Sicily, from Michael Corleone's refuge on the island in the original movie and the early life of Don Vito in *Part II*, to the final denouement on the steps of the Teatro Massimo in *Part III*. Unsurprisingly, these Palermo sequences brought the cast to The Palms where Al Pacino (who played Michael Corleone) left the sketch of a glass in Toti Librizzi's album and Coppola drew a book in honour of Mario Puzo's novel. Ironically, Coppola saw little mileage in turning the text into film when he was first approached about the project. As Puzo has himself admitted, *The Godfather* was nothing more than a money-maker for its author to support his large family, and was a book that he compared unfavourably with the two previous novels he had written. Coppola had the perception that the pulp elements of Puzo's work would clash with his art-house ethic and was thus dissuaded.

However, Coppola was in need of money due to the box office failure of previous projects. The director and his partner, George Lucas, owed huge sums to Warner Brothers. Realistically, he could not afford to turn down a potential money-spinner. Coppola was asked to work directly with Puzo on the script for the first movie which, surprisingly, resulted in a harmonious partnership. When the Italian-American community heard whisperings of the production, there were inevitable mutterings of opposition. Long tainted with the stigma of gangsterism, Americans of Italian descent were not keen to have this image reinforced. The Italian-American Civil Rights League contacted elected officials, asking them to persuade the studio heads to cancel the project. A degree of accommodation was reached when it was agreed that proceeds from the premiere would be directed towards community organisations.

If thought was given to the feelings of immigrant Italians, little heed was paid to the impact such a project would have on Sicilians, especially given that Coppola had insisted the Sicilian scenes be filmed on the island, thereby reinforcing the link already evident in the script. Although, after pressure from the aforementioned Civil Rights League, the words 'mafia' and '*Cosa Nostra*' do not appear in the film, it is obvious to all that the gangster families were implicitly part of such an organisation. The critical reception of the film and its sequel went beyond expectations in America, with the movie receiving multiple Academy Awards and Golden Globes. Coppola had achieved the considerable feat of taking a genre concept and creating a multi-layered film that interwove the complexities of immigrant struggle with a brutal realisation of the American Dream — from rural poverty to corporate gangsterism.

There were dissenters, however, who saw a bleak hopelessness in the stone-faced violence, especially that meted out by Michael Corleone, Don Vito's son, on his rise to control the organisation. Peter Cowie, in his biography of Coppola, quotes the director Nicholas Roeg, who found that Michael's murderous brutality in pursuit of power was full of dark fatality, lacking all decency — it was a film that kept him awake at night.

In many ways, the more troublesome aspect is the idealisation of certain figures, a pseudo-glamorisation that even pleased some members of the mob who must have been concerned about their portrayal in a mass-market film. At the start of *The Godfather*, Vito Corleone, aka Vito Andolini, is holding court in the manner of a medieval monarch. He is being petitioned by those who seek the kind of justice that cannot be administered via the forces of law and order. Vito's manners are courteous and civilised in direct contrast to those who, in real life, have been recorded by the police. Their speech, littered with vicious invective, is anything but the well-mannered politesse of Corleone's latent threats.

In his book *Cosa Nostra*, the historian John Dickie gives his views on the clash between the fiction of cinema and the reality of organised crime. He acknowledges the veracity of certain aspects but also highlights the stylisation that leads to a warping of the truth. Dickie tells the story of the respected surgeon Dr Galati, who was the first to leave a detailed account of the mafia persecution he experienced in the 1870s. Dr Galati managed, on behalf of his family, a fruit farm that was situated on the edge of Palermo. The previous owner, his brother-in-law, had been threatened by the farm warden, Carollo, who was syphoning off profits from the sale of the citrus fruit. Galati, not wanting further trouble, decided to lease the property to a third party, only to find that such a proposal enraged Carollo, who warned him not to pursue this course of action.

The surgeon promptly sacked the presumptuous guard and hired a new man who was subsequently found with bullets in his back. Galati went to the police and hired yet another warden. The police were ineffective and Galati's family and employees continued to be threatened. Once more, the new guard was shot, although this time he survived and reported the perpetrators to the police. Suspecting that the police inspector was in league with Carollo, and realising what he was up against, Galati fled with his family to Naples, after which the original warden, backed by powerful friends, casually applied for a permit to go hunting on the Galati family property. This event is illustrative of the nascent mafia in action — a far cry from the magnanimous mumblings of Corleone, distributing his largesse to those in his thrall. Dickie notes that the code of honour which applied in the Galati case, linked to an initiation ritual, is a far cry from that widely held in everyday circles.

Marlon Brando, who was cast in the role of Don Vito, wore a plastic mouth insert to ensure a consistent emulation of his poorly enunciated speech. The characters were spellbound in both respect and fear of the Don, and in many ways, the same could be said of the actors with regard to Marlon Brando, with whom they all wanted to perform. It took days for their awestruck timidity to subside, helped along by Brando's comic expressions designed to put them at ease. Brando also went the extra mile for his part, as Stefan Kanfer records in his biography of the actor, by attending a dinner at the house of a renowned *mafioso*. He internalised the feeling of family, in both senses of the word. Al Pacino, whose grandparents actually hailed from Corleone, has also admitted to meeting mob figures to better characterise his portrayal of Don Vito's son Michael but, understandably, has been very cagey in giving away any details. Interestingly, Mario Puzo claimed never to have met a real gangster in his life.

In the first film, released in 1972, Michael Corleone flees to Sicily, where he seeks shelter after his killing of Virgil Sollozzo and a corrupt police officer; the event triggers a full-blown mafia war. Sollozzo was seeking investment and protection for his drug-trafficking venture, a business that Vito Corleone was wary of entering for fear of upsetting his political connections. As we know from the mafia summit at The Palms, the real organisation was less chary of dealing with illicit substances. Post-war *mafiosi* on both sides of the Atlantic were already dipping more than their toes into the lucrative heroin market.

When on the island, Michael inevitably goes to Corleone, which was represented by the Messinese village of Forza d'Agrò, a settlement at the opposite end of Sicily. Its narrow stone-paved streets and traditional buildings were deemed to be more like Corleone than the town itself. Nearby Savoca also stood in for the infamous childhood home of Don Vito. Unlike the American critical reception of the film, the Italian press originally had a mixed reaction, particularly with regard to the elements shot in Sicily. John Dickie recalls one critic dubbing the Sicilian scenes 'offensively stupid'. Dickie agrees with this opinion, to a certain extent, especially when he cites Michael querying the lack of men in Corleone, to which he receives the response that it was due to the ubiquity of vendetta. The historian then makes the point that typhus was the more likely killer during that time period.

The Godfather Part II followed on the successful heels of *Part I* in 1974, with Robert De Niro playing the younger Vito Corleone. Once again, Forza d'Agrò hosted the Sicilian segments. When Vito returns to the island for the first time after emigrating, he exacts revenge on the local mafia chieftain who had killed his family. Corleone's arrival in Palermo was not actually shot in the city but at a small rural railway station among the foothills of Etna which caused much delay in filming due to the constant cloud cover descending from the mountain.

The Godfather Part III (1979) is the film with the closest connection to Palermo and The Palms. Michael's son, Anthony, has become an opera tenor and is given the opportunity to debut at the Teatro Massimo. It is thanks to Coppola's insistence on shooting in authentic locations that some of the cast and crew decamped to the island and spent time in the hotel. It takes less than ten minutes to amble from the hotel foyer to the steps of the theatre, although we imagine Pacino *et al* were provided with cars. Pip Whitaker's Villa Malfitano was also featured, as were a wider plethora of Sicilian locations including Segesta, Taormina and the hilltop town of Erice — reflecting Coppola's significantly increased budget.

The film, despite Academy Award nominations, did not reach the critical heights of its forebears. The fact that it was the third and final part of a trilogy caused one of the major issues. It is difficult to fully understand the motivations of the characters and intricacies of plot development in the movie without having seen and recalled the first two films. In addition, the acting of Sofia Coppola in the role of Michael's daughter Mary is, at best, flat, with no romantic connection emanating from the scenes between her and Andy Garcia, who plays Sonny Corleone's illegitimate son Vincent.

Sofia is central to the finale; as the curtain falls on the opera inside the Massimo, it also falls on Mary Corleone's life as she takes a bullet from an assassin that was meant for her father. The choice of opera was no coincidence. Coppola deliberately chose *Cavalleria rusticana* by Mascagni, which on the surface is a simple Sicilian tale of mistrust, honour and revenge based on a Giovanni Verga story. The opera title translates as 'rustic chivalry' — a concept that the mafia have always wanted to own and project to the wider public. 'Rustic chivalry' is precisely the ambient mood that floats through the early scenes of *The Godfather* as Don Vito holds court; it embodies his value system and his sense of judgement — a chivalry based on honour that maintains a deadly threat for those who transgress. *Cavalleria rusticana* manufactured this myth of a ritualistic world ruled by these homespun values of honour and violence, far from the octopus-like organisation the mafia was already becoming.

Many who have written on the mafia's origins have commented on the popularity of the *Cavalleria*. Dickie is sure of its influence in diverting the public from the organisation's real threat. Roberto M. Dainotto, in his book *The Mafia: A Cultural History*, reflects on Coppola's choice of music to accompany the final moments of the trilogy, a series that he, perhaps, had grown weary of furthering. For Dainotto, either consciously or otherwise, Coppola had ended his cultural contribution to the mafia myth with the music that triggered its inception. The aged and blind Michael Corleone fades away to the strains of the *Intermezzo* from the very opera that nostalgically paints a world where men behave with codified honour, enacting their own law in a society that has left them to their own devices.

Coppola's films have indeed become a cultural phenomenon, but one that has left Sicily synonymous with the image of Vito Andolini in his guise as Marlon Brando's Don Corleone. Cross the road from the entrance to The Palms and take any side street with a souvenir shop and it is extremely likely that the vision of Brando's distorted face will appear on anything from a T-shirt, tea towel or ashtray to a cigarette lighter. It might seem that this type of merchandise is essential to a healthy tourist trade when so many foreign visitors have this film as a point of reference, but there is a horrible irony in the marketing of such trinkets. The shops that display and sell Brando's image — the image of a man who embodies the concept of mafia protection — will be paying the *pizzo*, the local word for protection money.

It prompts the question as to why any Sicilian would want to glorify and promulgate a topic that has so dented the island's image. One answer can be found in the reflected glory of Hollywood success, which works on the principle that any publicity is good publicity and that the spotlight is enough of a draw, irrespective of the subject matter that lies beneath the surface. Don Corleone's 'rustic chivalry' is a nod to the past, albeit stylised, which has created a stasis worthy of Lampedusa's timeworn Prince Salina, the man who warned of upstart *mafiosi* like Don Calogero.

There are locals who boycott establishments that market Brando to tourists, but Sicily has clearly not escaped the drip feed of *Godfather* associations embedded in our collective psyche. During a food festival in a hill town near Palermo, we fell into conversation with a group of twenty-something Sicilians. Talk turned to dialect and representations of the island in world cinema. Their first point of reference for the use of the Sicilian language in a popular film was De Niro in *The Godfather Part II*. One of your authors was wearing a black waistcoat and it was at this point in the conversation that three of the young men, who were university-educated, turned to each other and pointed at the garment. With admiring glances, they muttered that it resembled the attire sported by De Niro in the film. There was no irony or gentle teasing — just an observational respect for Coppola's work.

It is even more surprising that these impressions linger when events in the 1980s and 1990s shattered any remaining notions of the mafia as anything other than an open wound, a complex criminal organisation regularly infected with drug money from America. Heroin became even bigger business and the money generated had to go somewhere for laundering purposes. Financial scandals ensued that even reached the hallowed turf of the Vatican and its banking interests when the financier Michele Sindona ('The Shark') and the banker Roberto Calvi ('God's Banker') both died in mysterious circumstances. Sindona was already serving a life sentence for murder after having been previously convicted of perjury, fraud and the mismanagement of funds. He died in prison from cyanide that had found its way into his coffee. In 1982, Calvi was found dangling from scaffolding under Blackfriars Bridge in London, a supposed suicide. Later investigations revealed the suicide to have been staged — the choice of Blackfriars was undoubtedly symbolic, since Calvi was a member of P2, a pseudo-masonic lodge whose members referred to themselves as the *frati neri*, the 'black friars'.

As the banking scandals became front page news, the Sicilian mafia was engaged in a ruthless internal fight to the death that saw the Corleonesi family establish ultimate control. Hundreds died in the Second Mafia War including many so-called *cadaveri eccellenti* (literally, the excellent cadavers), in other words, those who died whilst holding significant positions in the state apparatus, notably the politicians Piersanti Mattarella and Pio La Torre. Both these men were involved in the fight against the mafia, with Mattarella trying to put an end to corruption in the building industry and Pio La Torre promoting the mafia conspiracy law. General Carlo Alberto Dalla Chiesa was another casualty of the conflict. He had been sent to Palermo in 1982 with the specific task of stopping the violence. His car was forced off the road by armed gunmen on motorbikes and the occupants, including his bodyguard and wife, were riddled with bullets.

Some *mafiosi*, known as *pentiti*, broke ranks and enabled the judiciary to fight back. *Pentito* translates as 'penitent' or 'repentant', although those who turned state's evidence were more likely to be fearful for their lives than repentant of their crimes. One judge in particular, Giovanni Falcone, knew the value of these testimonies and, perhaps more importantly, the means of eliciting them. Falcone had grown up in the La Kalsa district of Palermo where he would have mixed with all levels of Palermitan society. He knew the mafia mindset and could converse on their level. Using Pio La Torre's law that made mafia association illegal, and with the help of *pentiti* like Tommaso Buscetta, he was able to build a strong case against the mafia leadership. Working alongside him was Paolo Borsellino, another crusading judge who also grew up in La Kalsa.

By 1986 the anti-mafia pool of judges was ready to prosecute hundreds of defendants in what became known as the maxi-trial. Scores of journalists, both national and international, descended on The Palms, turning the hotel's public spaces into an ante-courtroom. Reporters littered the foyer, urgently scribbling notes, talking into dictaphones and anticipating the events to come. The day's proceedings were mulled over with a glass of wine or whisky from Librizzi's bar. The judicial attack on the mafia was unprecedented, which took great courage, and the press knew they were reporting a momentous story.

The real courtroom was a specially constructed bunker inside Palermo's Ucciardone prison. High-level security and bullet-proof glass was much in evidence, but the effort proved worthwhile as the maxi-trial led to 360 convictions. However, rather than dissuade the Corleonesi from their path of violence, the trial merely provoked them further. *Cadaveri eccellenti* continued to fall including Salvo Lima, the ex-Mayor of Palermo and member of the European Parliament who was gunned down in 1992 on his way from Mondello, a beach resort near the city. Lima was not an anti-mafia warrior, but a politician who had been linked with the Sack of Palermo and the accompanying building contracts issued without due process. Lima was part of the faction in the Christian Democrat Party that supported Giulio Andreotti. Historians such as John Dickie have reported testimony from *pentiti* that claim Lima was assassinated because he had not kept promises regarding the lessening of sentences handed out during the maxi-trial.

Two months after the death of Lima, the whole of Italy was shocked by an incident that would impact Italians in much the same way that the death of John F. Kennedy affected Americans. People can tell you where they were and what they were doing when the news filtered through. Giovanni Falcone, exhausted by his constant battle with *Cosa Nostra* in his homeland, had accepted a post in Rome where he had effectively set up district offices designed to combat organised crime. He had also been instrumental in blocking a review of sentences for those convicted in the maxi-trial. On 23 May, Falcone took a car from the island's airport at Punta Raisi and was travelling home when the road beneath him erupted at Capaci. The escort car containing three police agents was thrown from the road, killing all inside. Falcone and his wife, Francesca Morvillo, were ejected through their windscreen with no hope of survival. The explosion, which registered on earthquake-monitoring equipment, was no natural phenomenon, but a bomb planted by the mafia.

When fellow judge Paolo Borsellino heard the news, he knew his days were numbered. The events after Falcone's assassination are immortalised in the film *The 57 Days*, a reference to the amount of time left to Borsellino. Luca Zingaretti, of Inspector Montalbano fame, plays the magistrate, who kept a red notebook detailing all his investigations on his person at all times. Borsellino was at the time in conversation with a *pentito* that he had visited in Rome, during which he was told of two supposedly corrupt officials. Before he had a chance to investigate further, he was assassinated in Palermo's Via D'Amelio where he was visiting his mother. The explosion from the nearby car also killed his bodyguards, amongst whom was Emanuela Loi, the first female police protection officer ever to be appointed in Italy. The red notebook disappeared from the scene. Investigations into Borsellino's murder are still ongoing and have centred on collusion between the state and *Cosa Nostra*.

In 1993, the Corleonesi boss Totò Riina was finally apprehended in Palermo after twenty-three years on the run. Nicknamed 'Shorty' or 'The Beast', Riina had been in hiding throughout the events of these years. From his redoubt, he had orchestrated the tentacle-like branches of an organisation that had infiltrated many aspects of society. The man who became the *de facto* boss once Riina had been jailed was Bernardo Provenzano, who had been a fugitive for even longer. Provenzano's reign saw less violence directed at the State. Despite his need to constantly move from place to place, he maintained control of operations through *pizzini*, small notes coded via, of all things, passages in the Bible. The notes were hand-delivered to the people that mattered. Provenzano was eventually arrested in 2006 by the police who had tracked a lorry delivering the laundry that had recently driven away from his family home. His hideout was remarkably close to Corleone.

The momentous events of 1992 took place during the premiership of Giulio Andreotti (1919–2013), one of Italy's longest-serving political figures. Andreotti was a native of Lazio and attended school and university in Rome. Having graduated in law, his political career took off when he became a member of the National Council of the newly-formed Christian Democrats in 1944. During the 1950s and 1960s, Andreotti held a number of ministerial positions, eventually becoming Prime Minister for the first time in 1972 and then again in 1976. His third tenure ended in June 1992 when he resigned at the end of the legislature. Newly made a Senator for Life, Andreotti decided to stand for the presidency of the Italian Republic. The presidential election took place in the wake of the assassination of Falcone and those members of parliament and deputies entitled to vote veered away from the old warrior, plumping instead for the compromise candidate, Oscar Luigi Scalfaro.

The taint of scandal was now beginning to dog Andreotti's footsteps. It was Salvo Lima's death that raised some serious questions for the former Prime Minister. The judiciary started to wonder how much he knew of Lima's dubious connections. In 1993 Andreotti was put on trial in Palermo for mafia association. The document published by the Public Prosecutor's Office and detailing the introductory exposition from the criminal proceedings specifically mentions Lima but, of particular interest to us, it also cites meetings held at The Palms between two very wealthy Sicilian businessmen, Antonio and Ignazio Salvo, and Christian Democrat politicians. The Salvos, who were cousins, had been prosecuted for mafia association in the maxi-trial. Antonio died of natural causes during the trial, whilst Ignazio was convicted and later assassinated.

The prosecution document goes on to state that one of The Palms' barmen often saw the Salvos in the hotel where they kept a suite. The cousins met with Lima and also with other local politicians from the east of the island, some of whom would stay at the establishment on a regular basis when in Palermo. Lima came to the hotel specifically with the aim of seeing the Salvos together with the others. The prosecution alleged that the Salvos' conversation included exhortations to the politicians that they fulfil certain tasks which the cousins had already committed themselves to achieving.

Andreotti denied ever meeting the Salvos, despite the fact that images of the businessmen and the politician were produced during the trial. The initial verdict of the court in 1999 completely acquitted him, but the prosecution took the case to the Court of Appeal, where the final decision was delivered in 2003. The appeal judges stated that Andreotti had made himself available to the mafia until the spring of 1980, after which he had demonstrated a commitment to the anti-mafia cause. The time-frame stated was an important factor as Italy's statute of limitations meant that older prosecutions would lapse beyond a certain date, therefore Andreotti was exonerated. He was also cleared in another trial in Perugia, where he was charged with complicity in the murder of journalist Mino Pecorelli who was thought to have information that could destroy his political career. The prosecution case, that the mafia had killed Pecorelli for Andreotti, was upheld on appeal but finally dismissed through lack of evidence by the Court of Cassation.

Whether Andreotti was or was not guilty, he was the epitome of a Machiavellian politician. Throughout his career, he attracted many caustic nicknames, amongst which were *Belzebù* (Beelzebub), the Black Pope, the Sphinx, Moloch and the Hunchback. It was Bettino Craxi, his political opponent, who coined the first devilish epithet which is somewhat ironic given that Craxi fled Italy to avoid corruption charges. The most evocative sobriquet attached to Andreotti is *Il Divo* — literally, the divine one — which became the title of Paolo Sorrentino's acclaimed film that portrayed the politician's life. The term is associated with celebrity but, in this context, there is a nuanced sarcasm alluding to his remarkable political survival.

Throughout his career, Andreotti had occasionally stayed at The Palms. In an interview with Toti Librizzi, the author Egidio Morici asked the barman if it was true that the politician used to enter the hotel through the main entrance and leave through a secondary exit in order to meet people in secret, leading everyone to believe that he was still in his hotel room. Such rumours were commonplace for a man of Andreotti's reputation for political cunning and gnomic behaviour.

Librizzi refuted the claim, but went on to illustrate Andreotti's character by telling Morici that he had refused to draw a design in his autograph book; instead writing, 'To Toti, Giulio Andreotti, hopeless at drawing'. This was a charismatic way of being self-deprecating whilst avoiding the request. Librizzi says that the politician considered art a special talent that he did not possess. During the time of Andreotti's trial, the actor and cabaret performer Oreste Lionello was staying at The Palms. In response to Librizzi's usual request for a doodle, the performer drew a caricature of Andreotti and wrote '*a piede libero*' which can be translated as 'on the loose' or 'on the run'.

Senator for Life, Giulio Andreotti died at the age of ninety-four in 2013 from respiratory problems. His incredibly long political career led one journalist to ask him whether being in power was wearing him out. Always ready with a quick rejoinder, he replied, 'power wears out those who don't have it'. As noted by author Peter Bondanella, this bitter truism found its way into the mouth of Calò, a corrupt banker in *The Godfather Part* III, whispered into the ear of master criminal Lucchesi as Calò stabs him in the neck. Coppola may have had one eye on political developments in Italy, but he was too removed, as an American, to analyse matters from the inside. The film director Francesco Rosi (1922–2015) however had the advantage of proximity and experience.

Rosi was born in Naples and found fame with his cinematic portrayal of the Mattei oil scandal, as well as his aforementioned depiction of Salvatore Giuliano. In 1990, he released *Dimenticare Palermo* (*Forgetting Palermo*), a film loosely based on Edmonde Charles-Roux's 1966 book *Oublier Palerme*. In collaboration with the writers Gore Vidal and Tonino Guerra, he took some of Charles-Roux's plot lines and liberally interspersed them with his own Sicilian content, including a hotel and its manager, a mysterious aristocratic resident, an American politician with a radical drug policy and mafia men with too many vested interests. Rosi knew the history of The Palms and the enigmatic Baron Di Stefano, and saw them as a perfect fit for his film, which would be released in the English-speaking world as *The Palermo Connection*.

As critics have pointed out, the film was incorrectly marketed as a thriller rather than a political exposé and there were some dubious casting decisions, especially the cut-glass Englishman Joss Ackland as the mafia boss and James Belushi as the lead character. The film's value lies in its ability to explore the connections between power and organised crime, raising questions of policy, corruption and society's fatalistic attitude to the issues concerned. Belushi plays the role of Carmine Bonavia, a candidate running for the Mayor of New York under the slogan, 'To Make a Difference'. One of his major initiatives is the opening of drug rehabilitation centres in poor neighbourhoods. On the campaign trail, he meets a female journalist from Palermo who provokes him into thinking more deeply about society's attitudes to drugs.

Realising he needs a major strategy to reverse his flagging position in the polls, he somewhat cynically adopts the policy of legalising drugs. His father, a Sicilian immigrant, is truly horrified, understanding that reprisals from the mafia, who control the extremely lucrative narcotics trade between Palermo and New York, would be swift and deadly. Bonavia tells his father to reassure the *mafiosi* who frequent his restaurant that the initiative is simply a vote catcher and he has no intention of putting it into practice once elected. The conversation with the Palermitan journalist also prompted Bonavia to cancel his forthcoming honeymoon to Venice in favour of rediscovering his family's roots in Sicily's capital.

Now riding high in the polls, the mayoral candidate and his new wife cross the Atlantic and check into the Grand Hotel which, although a set, is clearly intended to represent The Palms. The hotel manager Gianni Mucci, played by Philippe Noiret, takes the couple around his prestigious establishment, pointing out the bust of Wagner, a clear copy of the original in The Palms, and proudly tells them that the grand piano was last played by Rubenstein. As they step into the hotel's lounge, complete with its large television, Mucci turns to Bonavia and gestures towards a comfortable chair, saying that it was Lucky Luciano's favourite, where he would sit for hours watching TV.

Baron Di Stefano's doppelganger, referred to as 'the Prince', is played by a now aged Vittorio Gassman. He first makes an appearance on one of the hotel's terraces, tending to his caged birds, an obvious metaphor for his own gilded imprisonment. He tells Bonavia's wife that they are his family before going on to lament the passing of the hotel's golden years which saw visits from the crowned heads of Europe, now replaced by package tourists. Fascinated by such an unusual character, she asks the aristocrat if she can take a photograph of him outside the hotel where the light is better. He simply replies that he never goes outside the building. Subsequently, on meeting an American diplomat, the newly-weds learn the reason for the Prince's reticence — the self-same story attributed to Baron Di Stefano.

Mysteriously, during the first days of Bonavia's visit, bunches of white jasmine make a disturbing appearance, turning up at his dinner table, in his horse-drawn carriage and even in his hotel bedroom. It turns into an even more ominous threat when he realises that the delicate flower is very difficult to find during the hot summer weather. He becomes obsessed with tracking down the youth who first offered a bunch of these flowers to his wife whilst sitting at a café table. He believes the young man will be able to tell him who is behind these veiled threats. Subsequently, when eating octopus in the Vucciria, he spots the seller and corners him. As they start to fight, onlookers join in and, in the melee, the young man is stabbed with a knife belonging to a fishmonger — a brutal homage to Guttuso's famous painting. The blame falls on Bonavia, but the incident is clearly a setup. The jasmine seller is taken to hospital, fighting for his life.

Bonavia is told that he will face no charges if the youth survives as it will be classed as self-defence; however, if he dies, a trial and long sentence is on the horizon. The shaken politician retreats to the hotel where he has dinner with the Prince, who, clothed elegantly in white linen, recommends the dressed crab, claiming that he had taught the chef to make it in the finest English fashion. With throwaway *sang-froid*, he tells Bonavia that the jasmine vendor will surely die if 'they' want him out of the picture badly enough. As a knowing aside, Gassman's character turns the conversation to the heat and lack of jasmine. In a veiled piece of advice, he explains that the only source for the flower in such weather is near a spring on the way to Trapani.

Losing no time, Bonavia throws off his police minders and heads to the specified location where he encounters the mafia boss behind the threats. He asks him to let the young man live only to be told that he had already died an hour previously. The boss is emphatic that Bonavia will be tried for manslaughter and found guilty, implying the judiciary are in his pocket. He offers an alternative solution where the American politician's innocence is proven by irrefutable photographic evidence, on the condition that he drop any notion of legalising drugs — a policy that Bonavia had, ironically, come to believe in. With a new understanding and a defeatist attitude, the mayoral candidate returns to New York and embarks on reversing the manifesto commitment.

The camera cuts to Bonavia in New York, about to dig the first symbolic shovel of earth from the site of a new drug rehabilitation centre, thereby reverting to his former policy, which he now sees as futile but expedient. Belushi's character stands silent as his thoughts race and he passes the shovel to a nearby cleric, unable to proceed. He realises that he is breaking a promise to the *éminence grise* he had met in Sicily, a decision he will shortly pay for in a hail of bullets.

The film is very much of its time, the period at the end of the 1980s when Sicily was experiencing the worst excesses of mafia violence.

Rosi's plot, enlivened by Vidal's characteristically acerbic dialogue, is intended to examine the root causes of organised crime's hold on certain aspects of political and civil society. Although not entirely successful in achieving its aims, the film stands as an example of an *auteur* film director's attempt at laying bare a complex issue, whilst lacing his story with colourful vignettes taken from recent Sicilian folklore. The hotel and its resident prince are the steadfast witnesses to yet another convoluted human drama, a repetition of history they have sadly observed too many times before. In this, Rosi succeeded.

Sicily has, fortunately, left behind the extremes seen at this point in its history. A new wave of young, well-informed campaigners are starting to challenge the accepted price of accommodating the mafia. *Addiopizzo* is a movement that intends to confront the collection of protection money extorted from local businesses. Organisations that refuse the so-called *pizzo* now display the movement's logo in their shop or restaurant windows. Some of the products sold in these businesses are grown on land confiscated from convicted *mafiosi*, thereby creating a corruption-free cycle of production, manufacture and retail. The movement also works with local schoolchildren, educating them in a culture that promotes legality and an 'anti-racket' mentality.

The Palms, like its fictional counterpart, has witnessed the best and worst of its city's extremes. It is no surprise that film-makers and authors want to draw on the hotel's history as a plot device in their narratives. Gaetano Savatteri, the author who featured the tale of that other eccentric baron, La Lomia, in his book *I siciliani*, uses one more of the hotel's clandestine political meetings in his 2003 work *La ferita di Vishinskij* (*Vyshinsky's Wound*). The title refers to Stalin's prosecutor Andrei Vyshinsky who liaised with Sicily's Communist Party during World War II.

Vyshinsky (1883–1954) was one of the chief judicial figures in the dictator's Great Purge, the wave of repression that took place between 1936 and 1938 which targeted anyone deemed politically suspect, from Communist *apparatchiks* to unsuspecting peasants and army leaders — essentially, anyone thought to be a threat to Uncle Joe's leadership. Vyshinsky's rhetorical flourishes were laden with the most scathing language, designed to heap the utmost denigration on his foes. Trotsky's supporters were 'mad dogs' and enemies of the state were the 'dregs of society' and 'stinking carrion'.

After the Germans invaded the Soviet Union, the prosecutor was transferred from Moscow to Kuibyshev where he remained loyal to the leadership. Stalin rewarded him with an appointment to the Allied Control Council for Italian affairs. Initially, he busied himself with shipping former Russian POWs back to the Soviet Union, whether they wanted to go or not. As an Italian Communist movement began to gain a foothold in the political vacuum left by the collapse of Fascism, Vyshinsky saw an opportunity to liaise with his international brethren. He was trying to manoeuvre the local Communist Party into a dominant position, from which it could take advantage when Italy once again became a fully functioning constitutional state. Historians have analysed new documentation that has come to light and discovered that, at the time, the country's Communists were much in thrall to Stalin's Russia.

In December 1943, Vyshinsky turned his attention to Sicily. He asked the British how many Fascists had been tried and shot since the island had fallen to the Allies and was seemingly unimpressed to learn that a mere 1,500 were in prison. He descended on Palermo for a flying visit with the intention of bolstering Communism in Sicily whilst at the same time trying to avert moves towards an independent island. The man he met was Giovanni Montalbano, who had actively encouraged his visit. Some say that the pair reputedly met in a suite at The Palms. Gaetano Savatteri takes a novelist's liberty with the facts, interweaving Vyshinsky's visit with multiple semi-fictional plot lines revolving around the mysterious death of a young girl, Maddalena Pancamo, who disappeared from a ferry between Naples and Palermo in 1985.

Librarian Leonardo Lo Nardo decides to dig deeper into the events around Maddalena's death which leads him to a feud between the Pancamo and Pintacorona families and a conspiracy at The Palms in 1960, based on the true story of a scandalous meeting at the hotel. The scandal involved the politician Silvio Milazzo, who sought to squeeze the political middle ground by bringing together the unlikely bedfellows of left and right in a coalition government — in a political strategy termed *milazzismo* after him. His second term as President of the Sicilian Region was beginning to fall apart in 1960 as the Christian Democrats began to gain enough ground to take a majority. Ludovico Corrao, chief ideologue of the Sicilian Christian Social Union (UCSC), Milazzo's new party, and the Communist Vincenzo Marrano had identified Christian Democrats who they thought could be persuaded to jump ship and support Milazzo's government, one of whom was councillor and Mayor of Barcellona Carmelo Santalco.

Corrao and Marrano met Santalco in room 128 with the intention of offering suitable inducements, supposedly enough to sway the Mayor who spent his days as a stationmaster to prop up their majority in the Regional Assembly. They were unaware however that Santalco was a committed politician who was playing his own game. He had already reported the meeting to the future President of the Region, Giuseppe D'Angelo, who instigated the placing of microphones under Santalco's bed in order to record the conversation. The resultant uproar split apart Milazzo's government when the attempted bribery and corruption — involving 100 million lire — was revealed. Savatteri quotes newspaper reports in his book to lend authenticity to the story.

He sets Vyshinsky's meeting with Montalbano in the Hotel Excelsior, not The Palms, where Stalin's prosecutor is accompanied by Russian minders. As Vyshinsky shakes the hand of the Sicilian Communist, Savatteri adds the flourish of a gunshot that fells the lawyer, leaving his shirt impregnated with blood — a wound that seems to be far worse than it really is. Witnesses are summarily told by the Russian minders that the incident never happened. As the novel progresses, a man in the US claims to be Vyshinsky, despite the fact that he had actually died in 1954. He asserts that the death was staged so that he could disappear and avoid the possible retaliation of the Khrushchev government. Before an investigation can be conducted and the man identified via the wound on his chest, he commits suicide.

Savatteri's story is complex in its interplay between fact and fiction, knotting and loosening numerous threads to invite the reader into this multi-layered tale of corruption and intrigue. The fact that The Palms was the chosen location for the real-life meeting upon which Savaterri's fiction is modelled is no coincidence — the building is a physical manifestation of Palermo's tortuous history, a silent witness to the machinations of duelling aristocrats, Fascist agents, spies, corrupt politicians, the representatives of organised crime and Cold War warriors, not to mention hedonistic writers and actors. Such a rich and famous, if not infamous, history made the outcry even greater when it was mooted in 2013 that The Palms might be closing its doors for good.

Toti Librizzi was so dismayed by this turn of events that he was moved to write an open letter which was published in the newspaper *La Repubblica* under the title 'Salvate il mio Hotel delle Palme' ('Save my Palms Hotel'). In fact, the proposed closure made a considerable splash in all Sicily's local papers from Ragusa in the south-east to the Aeolian Islands in the Tyrrhenian Sea as well as other national dailies such as *La Stampa*. Statements came from the regional government that they could not simply stand by and watch the demise of such an iconic institution, not to mention the loss of so many jobs.

The company that owned The Palms, Acqua Marcia, was looking to reorganise its Sicilian assets and had formally notified the hotel sector's leading body, Federalberghi, that it intended to close the hotel. Despite the fact that Federalberghi had recorded increasing visitor numbers to Palermo in the year preceding the announcement, the gap between The Palms' income and the cost of running the establishment was still deemed too wide. Crisis meetings were held in December 2013. Librizzi compared the closure to being evicted from his own home, despite having retired some years previously. He spoke for many Palermitans when he lamented the planned demise in emotive and plaintive terms, feeling that the hotel's end would be yet another blow to the fabric of the city's history. His most poignant remark sums up the hotel's impact in a more heartfelt manner than any journalist or historian could achieve: 'The *albergo* at 398 Via Roma is the crossroads through which much of twentieth-century culture has passed.'

He urged the city's governmental institutions to rally in defence of the venerable establishment in which he had lent a confidential ear to many at his bar whose 'secrets surfaced in whisky glasses'. The writer Leonardo Sciascia, who we know concerned himself with an investigation into the demise of the French author Raymond Roussel, was one of Librizzi's friendly customers and one who referred to the barman as his colleague — both men were students of the human condition and understood their motivations and manoeuvres. This is quite a compliment coming from the lips of a man of Sciascia's stature, known, as he was, for his piercing insight. From his exposure of mafia *omertà* in *The Day of the Owl* to his work focusing on the death of Aldo Moro, or the historical resonances of *The Council of Egypt*, in which a fake history of Arab-Sicily is discovered, Sciascia had always been a man of conscience concerned with the vagaries of his island condition.

Librizzi, as if a character in one of Sciascia's novels, questioned the unbelievable prospect of ending The Palms' long and rich history with emptiness, a vacuum, a cul-de-sac from which it would never emerge. The appeals from the hotel's famous barman and many others with respect for its cultural value did not fall on deaf ears. By the following February, things were beginning to look up. Acqua Marcia came to an agreement with the *Ufficio Provinciale del Lavoro* (Regional Labour Office) and the unions, negotiating a compromise deal to minimise redundancies with some staff sacrificing full-time for part-time hours. Although not satisfactory to all parties, it meant that the hotel's doors could stay open.

The *La Repubblica* article in which Toti Librizzi made his plea features him in a photograph from the 1970s with the ballerina, Carla Fracci. Both are smiling, standing in front of row upon row of bottles — everything from VAT 69 to Chivas Regal. Such an eclectic range of beverage choice was one of the casualties when the hotel emerged from its struggle to stay open. The alcove-like bar, situated up a small flight of stairs behind the foyer, became a ghost of its former self. The wood-framed shelving, inlaid with mirrors, remained, but there was little else left that gave a clue to its past identity. Gone were the chairs and low, round tables, replaced by a display cabinet protecting some scant reminders of the hotel's former glories, including a signed photo of Raymond Roussel. Although a small whisper of The Palms' past, one cannot help but feel that the space would be a fitting home to Toto Librizzi's *Casa museo della memoria*, where the memorabilia could eloquently speak for itself in the surroundings that prompted its collection.

The hotel is no longer part of the Acqua Marcia/AMT group and has been taken over by Algebris who, at the time of writing, have temporarily closed the doors for renovation with an opening date of 2020. Before its closure, walking the public spaces of the reprieved hotel felt akin to mixing with the transient spirits of the past. The Blue

Room (Sala Azzura), sometimes referred to as the Palmetta restaurant, was often empty apart from a large round table in the centre, and a few comfortable chairs pushed to the edges, ready to be positioned at a moment's notice should the occasion arise. The low hum of diners chattering over their food was difficult to conjure in the elegant silence, yet, strangely, the hushed atmosphere lent itself to the vivid picture of an Ingham-Whitaker moving aside the gilt mirror that still hides the passageway leading to the Anglican Church opposite. Clearly, Baron Di Stefano would have known about this secret tunnel and perhaps considered its opportunities whilst dining with the rich and famous. Vittorio Gassman springs to mind, playing the role of the Prince in The Palermo Connection in which he laments a passing world, replaced by mass tourism.

The snob in Gassman's aristocrat would have been horrified to see guests at the breakfast buffet in the magnificent surroundings of the Sala Specchi, wearing Bermuda shorts and baggy T-shirts. The Sala has undoubtedly been one of Palermo's most glamorous backdrops in which to take an early morning brioche, juice and cappuccino. The individual tables were still laid with fine white linen draped over golden underskirts in the futile expectation of receiving a nobleman or film star. Sadly, for much of the day the room remained in shadow, but a member of staff would happily flip the switches to reveal the play of light and reflection. The harshness of electric bulbs, however, would also highlight patches of wear on the pink wallpaper, as if the candles of yesteryear had guttered to a sooty end.

As your authors walked the halls in search of those magical numbers that harboured the hotel's secrets, we realised it was a somewhat fruitless exercise. The bland exterior of room 224 would not have witnessed the demise of Raymond Roussel and rooms 24, 25 and 26 had nothing to do with the birth of *Parsifal*. Regrettably, the years saw a renumbering of the hotel suites although the composer's name lived on in the Sala Wagner, used for conferences and meetings. The room was regimented with rows of straight-backed chairs in corporate red, all facing towards the long table at the front where the chairperson or speaker of the day would be stationed. Nothing quite removes the romance of an artistic locale as much as the commercial uniformity of modern-day business. A cut-glass chandelier hovered over the sea of chairs, imposing its seniority and provenance.

Survival has dictated a degree of accommodation with the needs of international business but, with rose-tinted spectacles, it is easy to forget that The Palms has always been intricately associated with people of commercial instinct. After all, it was Benjamin Ingham's entrepreneurial spirit that enabled its creation and the Florio family were frequent visitors during their period of dominance and expansion. The Belle Époque designs of Ernesto Basile were as much the setting for a business deal as the sleek chrome and glass which witness the corporate exchanges of today. Whispered encounters once saw the transfer of considerable sums between interested parties, occasionally ignoring the letter of the law according to the current tenets of the Guardia di Finanza.

Not all of the events held in the hotel's hallowed halls were so tasteless in nature. A swift perusal of recent activities prior to the renovation reveals the establishment's role as a cultural hub. Damiano Calabrese organised an event called Amor librorum, using The Palms as an exhibition space for the display of books of considerable antiquity, including the remarkable *Annali della felice città di Palermo* (*Annals of the Happy City of Palermo*) by Agostino Inveges, printed in 1649. The same organiser has also promoted the exposition of nineteenth-century engravings and traveller's tales from foreign authors who wrote about Sicily during the same era.

Occasionally, the hotel's displays are self-referential, as was the case with the 2018 initiative simply entitled 'Raymond', an homage to Raymond Roussel who breathed his last in 1933. The project was created by Luca Trevisani and counted on the collaboration of the German conceptual artist, Olaf Nicolai, who wrote to twenty-nine international authors and artists, inviting them to participate. Activities included a reading of *The Punk*, a Gideon Sams novel by contemporary artist Aleksandra Mir, with the added twist that she sat on the bed in her hotel room dressed in pyjamas and expected all her guests to be similarly attired. Other lucky guests were able to find a napkin embroidered with a capital 'R' at their breakfast table, or to receive a printed drawing from Ute Müller enclosed with their hotel invoice.

One of the more macabre exhibits was from Massimo Bartolini who displayed a large black and white print in room 121 which was a pseudo-technical architectural design, a method of killing oneself, which he named 'Suicide Machine'. Michael Dean chose to suspend a billiard tablecloth on frames in room 347, a reference to Roussel's method of writing which he elaborated in the text *How I Wrote Certain of My Books*. As briefly touched upon previously (see chapter 3), the Frenchman would take the word 'billard', for example, and its rhyming pair 'pillard' (looter), and then add similar words which would lead two almost identical sentences in different directions. A further creative twist came from Lucia Amara who designed postcards dedicated to Roussel's travels that were distributed widely throughout the rooms and corridors of the establishment.

Trevisani and Nicolai's vision turned the entirety of The Palms into a surprising gallery of reminiscence and modern reinterpretation. It was a fitting stage for such an original idea, an autodidactic labyrinth of rediscovery and reformation, proving that the slow demise of this esteemed venue is far from inevitable. It is to be hoped that the renovations of 2019–20 will reinvigorate this icon of Palermitan life, whilst honouring the essence of its unique heritage. Like an aged aristocrat, clinging to life through lack of an heir, The Palms, one of Palermo's epic bastions of the Belle Époque, faces an uncertain path. It will have to continue the task of reinvention in a century with which it seems to be increasingly at odds. Ultimately, the building's charm does not lie wholly in its fabric, but rather in its ghosts — the less tangible elements of its history that may yet give it a future.

BIBLIOGRAPHY

Abba, G.C., *The Diary of One of Garibaldi's Thousand*, trans. Vincent, E.R.,
Oxford University Press, Oxford, 1962

Alpert, M., 'The Spanish civil war and the Mediterranean', *Mediterranean
Historical Review*, vol 13, 1998

Anile, A., and Giannice, M.G., *Operazione Gattopardo*, Feltrinelli, Milan, 2013

Anonymous, *Review of the Neapolitan Sulphur Question*, 1840

Arcara, S., *Oscar Wilde e la Sicilia: temi mediterranei nell'estetismo inglese*,
Cavallotto, Catania, 1998

Balistreri, R., *Alchimia e architettura: Un percorso tra le ville settecentesche di
Bagheria*, Falcone, Bagheria, 2008

Basile, G., *Palermo è...*, Dario Flaccovio Editore, Palermo, 2013

Baxter, J., *De Niro: A Biography*, Harper Collins, London, 2003

Bicknell, A.S., *In the Track of the Garibaldians Through Italy and Sicily*, George
Manwaring, London, 1861

Bondanella, P., *Hollywood Italians: Dagos, Palookas, Romeos, Wise Guys and
Sopranos*, Continuum, New York, 2006

Borch, Le Comte de, *Lettres sur la Sicilie et sur l'île de Malthe*, Les Freres
Reycends, Turin, 1782

Borges, J.L., *Evaristo Carriego*, Alianza Editorial, Madrid, 1998

Bosworth, R.J.B., *Mussolini*, Arnold, London, 2002

Bozzacchi, G., *My Life in Focus: A Photographer's Journey with Elizabeth Taylor and
the Hollywood Jet Set*, University Press of Kentucky, Lexington, 2017

Bragg, M., *Rich: The Life of Richard Burton*, Hodder & Stoughton, London, 2010

Brydone, P., *Travels in Sicily and Malta*, George Clark & Son, Aberdeen, 1843

Callow, S., *Being Wagner: The Triumph of the Will*, William Collins, London, 2017

Calvino, I., *The Castle of Crossed Destinies*, Vintage Classics, London, 1998

Caruso, A., *I Siciliani*, Neri Pozza Editore, Vicenza, 2014

Charles-Roux, E., *Olvidar Palermo*, Ediciones G.P., Barcelona, 1969

Chirico, G. de, *Memorie della mia vita*, Bompiani, Milan, 2008

Churton, T., *Aleister Crowley: The Biography*, Watkins Publishing, London, 2011

Costanzo, E., *The Mafia and the Allies: Sicily 1943 and The Return of the Mafia*, trans. Lawrence, G., Enigma Books, New York, 2007

Cowie, P., *Coppola*, André Deutsch, London, 2013

Crowley, A., *The Diary of a Drug Fiend*, Samuel Weiser, York Beach, 1970

Dennis, G., *A Handbook for Travellers in Sicily*, John Murray, London, 1864

Dickie, J., *Cosa Nostra: A History of the Sicilian Mafia*, Hodder and Stoughton, London, 2007

Duggan, C., *The Force of Destiny: A History of Italy Since 1796*, Penguin, London, 2008

Dummett, J., *Palermo: City of Kings, The Heart of Sicily*, I.B. Tauris, London, 2015

Edwards, A. and Edwards, S., *Sicily: A Literary Guide for Travellers*, I.B. Tauris, London, 2014

Erhlich White, B., *Renoir: An Intimate Biography*, Thames & Hudson, London 2017

Ferrante, V., 'I segreti dell'Hotel des Palmes nelle dodici camere dei misteri', *La Repubblica* (15 March 2015)

Foucault, M., *Death and the Labyrinth*, Continuum, New York, 2006

Fountaine, M., *Love Among the Butterflies: Travels and Adventures of a Victorian Lady*, Penguin, London, 1982

Fusaro, P., *Palermo solo*, La fosse aux ours, Lyon, 2007

Getsy, D.J., *Sculpture and the Pursuit of a Modern Ideal in Britain, C. 1880–1930*, Ashgate, Farnham, 2004

Gilmour, D., *The Last Leopard: A Life of Giuseppe Tomasi di Lampedusa*, Collins-Harvill, London, 1990

Dainotto, R.M., *The Mafia: A Cultural History*, Reaktion Books, London, 2015

Grobel, L., *Al Pacino: The Authorized Biography*, Pocket Books, London, 2007

Hill, Rev. B., *Observations and Remarks in a Journey through Sicily and Calabria in the Year 1791*, John Stockdale, London, 1792

Kanfer, S., *Somebody: The Reckless Life and Remarkable Career of Marlon Brando*, Faber and Faber, London, 2008

Kirk, T., *The Architecture of Modern Italy, Volume I: The Challenge of Tradition, 1750–1900*, Princeton Architectural Press, New York, 2005

Lampedusa, G.T. di, *The Leopard*, trans. A. Colquhoun, Collins and Harvill Press, London, 1960

—— *The Siren & Selected Writings*, trans. A. Colquhoun, Harvill Press, London, 1995

Levy, S., *Dolce Vita Confidential: Fellini, Loren, Pucci, Paparazzi and the Swinging High Life of 1950s Rome*, Weidenfeld & Nicolson, London, 2018

Librizzi, T., *Il giardino di Colapesce*, http://ilgiardinodicolapesce.weebly.com/#, accessed 15 September 2018

— 'Salvate il mio Hotel delle Palme', *La Repubblica* (30 November 2013)

Lockhart Gordon, P., *Personal Memoirs or Reminiscences of Men and Manners at Home and Abroad Vol I*, Henry Colburn and Richard Bentley, London, 1830

Loren, S., *Yesterday, Today, Tomorrow: My Life*, Simon & Schuster, London, 2015

Macchia, G., *Il principe di Palagonia: mostri, sogni, prodigi nelle metamorfosi di un personnaggio*, Mondadori, Milan, 1979.

Marino, V., 'La storia del Barone Di Stefano tra leggende e misteri', *Castelvetrano News*, 2013, https://castelvetranonews.it/notizie/cultura/castelvetrano/la-storia-del-barone-di-stefano-tra-leggende-e-misteri/, accessed 23 October 2018

Maupassant, G. de, *Au Soleil or African Wanderings [and] La Vie Errante or In Vagabondia*, St Dunstan Society, Akron, OH, 1903

Maxwell, G., *God Protect Me from my Friends*, Pan Books, London, 1958

Miller, A., *Timebends: A Life*, Methuen, London, 1988

Molino, W., 'Le due rivali...', *La Domenica della Sera*, N. 14 (1956).

Moore, T. *The Poetical Works of Thomas Moore*, Bernh. Tauchnitz, Leipzig, 1842

Montero Sánchez, S., *El Barón y la niña eterna*, Editorial Círculo Rojo, Almería, 2014

Neu, I.D., 'An English Businessman in Sicily, 1806–1861', *Business History Review* Vol 31, No 4, Harvard, 1957

Newark, T., *The Mafia at War: the shocking true story of America's wartime pact with organized crime*, Greenhill Books, London, 2007

Lucky Luciano: Mafia Murderer and Secret Agent, Mainstream Publishing, Edinburgh, 2011

Newman, J.H., *Letters and Correspondence of John Henry Newman during his life in the English Church, edited, at Cardinal Newman's request, by Anne Mozley*, Longmans, Green, and Co., London, 1890

Norwich, J.J., *Sicily: A Short History from the Ancient Greeks to Cosa Nostra*, John Murray, London 2015

Ormonde, Marquis of, *An Autumn in Sicily*, Hodges and Smith, Dublin, 1850

Pirandello, L., *Novelle per un anno: Tutte le novelle di Pirandello*, Mauro Liistro Editore, Rome, 2017

Pitrè, G., *The Collected Sicilian Folk and Fairy Tales of Giuseppe Pitrè*, trans. and ed. by Zipes, J. and Russo, J., Routledge, New York, 2009

Procura della Repubblica, *Esposizione introduttiva del Pubblico Ministero nel processo penale n. 3538/94 N.R., instaurato nei confronti di Giulio Andreotti*, Direzione Distrettuale Antimafia, Palermo 1993

Quatriglio, G., *L'isola dei miti*, Flaccovio Editore, Palermo, 2009

Ragusa, E. (ed.), *Il naturalista siciliano: giornale di scienze naturali*, Oct. Ed., Stabilimento Tipografico Virzi, Palermo, 1881

Ragusa, E., *Catalogo ragionato dei coleotteri di Sicilia*, Stabilimento Tipografico Virzi, Palermo, 1883 — 'Coleotteri nuovi poco conosciuti della Sicilia', *Il naturalista siciliano: giornale di scienze naturali* Oct. Ed., 1881

Rodó, J.E., *Ariel*, trans. Sayers Peden, M., University of Texas Press, Austin, 1988

— *Viajes por Europa*, Linkgua-Digital, Barcelona, 2016

Savatteri, G., *I siciliani*, Laterza, Rome, 2006

— *La ferita di Vishinskij*, Sellerio, Palermo, 2009

Sciascia, L., *Atti relativi alla morte di Raymond Roussel*, Sellerio, Palermo, 2009

— *Actas relativas a la muerte de Raymond Roussel*, trans. Reija, J., Gallo Negro, Madrid, 2010

— *The Day of the Owl*, trans. Colquhoun, A. and Oliver, A., The New York Review of Books, New York, 2003

— *The Moro Affair and The Mystery of Majorana*, trans. Rabinovitch, S., Carcanet Press, Manchester, 1987

— *The Council of Egypt*, trans. Foulke, A., Apollo, London, 2016.

Serretta, C., *Alla scoperta dei segreti perduti della Sicilia*, Newton Compton Editori, Rome, 2016

Smith, J.V.C, MD (Ed), *The Boston Medical and Surgical Journal*, vol XII, D. Clapp, Jr., Boston, 1835

Stassinopoulos, A., *Maria Callas*, Hamlyn Paperbacks, Feltham, 1981

Trevelyan, R., *Princes Under the Volcano: Two Hundred Years of a British Dynasty in Sicily*, Phoenix Press, London, 2002

Velez-Giraldo, J.R., 'Newman's Mediterranean "Verses"', *Newman Studies Journal* vol 3:2, 2006

Villena, L.A. de, *El Gatopardo: La transformación y el abismo*, Gedisa, Barcelona, 2009

Verga, G. *Sicilian Stories: A Dual-Language Book*, trans. Appelbaum, S., Dover Publications, New York, 2003).

— *The House by the Medlar Tree*, trans. Craig, M., Harper & Brothers, New York, 1890

Wagner, C., trans Wagner, G., *Cosima Wagner's Diaries; Volume 2 1878–1883*, Harcourt Brace Jovanovich, San Diego, 1980

Whitaker, T., *Sicily and England: Political and Social Reminiscences 1848–1870*, A. Constable & Co Ltd, London, 1907

Wilde, O., *The Picture of Dorian Gray*, Wordsworth Editions, Ware, 1992

Zacco. M., *Il mondo in un cassetto al Grand Hotel delle Palme*, Edizioni Zacco, Palermo, 2015

ABOUT THE AUTHORS

Andrew Edwards is a writer and the translator of *Borges in Sicily*.
Suzanne Edwards trained in linguistics and is a dyslexia specialist. They
co-authored the acclaimed books *Sicily: A Literary Guide for Travellers*
and *Andalucia: A Literary Guide for Travellers*. In addition, they are authors
of *His Master's Reflection*, a journey in the footsteps of John Polidori,
Lord Byron's doctor.

INDEX